THE BASICS OF RETIREMENT

THE BASICS OF RETIREMENT
What You Need to Know to Plan for a Better Retirement

ISBN: 978-1-964046-95-2 (Paperback)
         978-1-964046-96-9 (Kindle eBook)

Editing by Tamma Ford
Copyediting by Lucy Spencer
Proofreading by Geena Barret
Text design and composition by Emily Fritz
Cover design by Casey Fritz

THE BASICS OF RETIREMENT

What You Need to Know to Plan for a Better Retirement

Raymond Bostian, LUTCF, CLTC
BOSTIAN RETIREMENT PLANNING
AND WEALTH MANAGEMENT

Christopher Wingler, CLTC
WINGLER WEALTH MANAGEMENT

DISCLOSURE

The information contained in this book is intended to provide helpful and informative material on the subject addressed. It is not intended to serve as a replacement for professional advice. Any use of the information in this book is at the reader's discretion.

The authors and publisher have made every reasonable effort to ensure the accuracy of the information contained in this book at the time of publication. They make no representations or warranties with respect to the completeness or accuracy of the contents and expressly disclaim any liability for any loss, damage, or disruption caused or alleged to be caused, directly or indirectly, by any errors or omissions, whether resulting from negligence or otherwise.

Clients' names, circumstances, and other personal information included in this book have been changed to protect privacy.

This publication is designed to provide accurate and authoritative information in regard to the subject matter covered. It is sold with the understanding that the publisher and authors are not engaged in rendering legal, tax, accounting, or other professional services. If legal advice or other expert assistance is required, the services of a competent professional should be sought.

Thank you for purchasing an authorized edition of this book and for complying with copyright law. No part of this book may be reproduced, stored in a retrieval system, or transmitted by any means, electronic, mechanical, photocopying, recording, or otherwise, without written permission from the copyright holder.

For ordering information or special discounts for bulk purchase, please contact events@bostianretirement.com.

Christopher Wingler, doing business as Wingler Wealth Management, offers Investment Advisory Services through Gradient Advisors, LLC (Arden Hills, MN 877-885-0508), an SEC Registered Investment Advisor. Gradient Advisors, LLC and its advisors do not render tax, legal, or accounting advice. Christopher Wingler is not a registered investment advisor and is independent of Gradient Advisors, LLC. Insurance products and services are offered through Christopher Wingler, independent agent. Christopher Wingler, Wingler Wealth Management, and Gradient Advisors, LLC are not affiliated with or endorsed by the Social Security Administration or any government agency.

Bostian Retirement Planning and Wealth Management and Raymond Bostian are not affiliated with Gradient Advisors, LLC.

CONTENTS

WHY READ OUR BOOK?

Our publisher asked us an interesting question: "You've been in business and highly successful for *decades*. Why are you only writing this book now?"

Two reasons.

First, it is to celebrate. As of January 2026, our firm is in its fiftieth year of continuous service to clients. This book is a celebration not just of our longevity as a professional services provider to our community but also of our love for what we do. We're not done yet—oh, no! We're not going anywhere anytime soon.

Second, a book gives us the opportunity to share some of our knowledge with a wider audience. We've trained and studied. However, our clients have also provided us with a wealth of knowledge over the years. Some of it has been cautionary—what not to do to prepare a successful retirement. We believe that learning *what not to do* is just as valuable as learning *what to do*.

In the course of our careers in retirement wealth planning with thousands of clients, both of us have observed that most people approaching their retirement date don't know the basics of retirement. We have found that far too many people think, "No worries, retirement will take care of itself." Maybe. But why chance it? That led Raymond, in his very first client meetings way back then, to become an educator. We have remained educators ever since. This book continues that legacy.

We could ask you right now, "What are the basics of a successful retirement?" and you would probably look at us like we're from planet Jupiter. By reading this book, you will learn what those basics are. They are "basic" because the topics we are going to talk about apply to just about everyone we have ever worked with.

If you really want a sneak peek at what "basic" means, here you go: What you will learn is how we work with you and every client to create a personalized retirement plan that protects your life savings, covers your essential and lifestyle expenses, and addresses your fear of running out of money.

And that is why you should read our book!

INTRODUCTION

Retirement, as we are living it today, is not just about leaving your job. It is, or should be, about living without constant financial fear, even though that old trusty paycheck is no longer there. The single greatest challenge to you as a retiree is ensuring that your savings, investments, and income sources don't run out before you do. This book is for your education so that you can meet that challenge with knowledge. That's first.

Next, it's about preserving your hard-earned money. That means identifying and understanding the financial risks you might have to face—and they can arise years into your retirement unless you plan. The education piece is to learn that there are ways to reduce and potentially even eliminate some of the risks we will present. That's second.

Finally, it's about planning wisely and strategically, so your money is always there for you. Our goal is to plan with you so that your money will fund all your needs in your later years—however long you live. In other words, we plan with you so that you have continuous streams of income for your whole life. That is third.

Raymond began in this business decades before even thinking about his own retirement. Imagine him as a twenty-something planner with sixty-something clients! But he spoke wisely to his often much older clients. He educated them. He presented solutions to them to keep their money safe. They trusted him. That's been the goal for both of us, along with our entire Bostian Retirement Planning and Wealth Management staff, for every single client.

Retirement can be the best part of your life. It should offer you the chance to do everything you dreamed of while you were working hard and saving money. You finally get the time to appreciate all the little things. You can focus on spending more time with your friends and family and pursuing all the hobbies you didn't have time for before retirement. You can realize some or all of those dreams.

But there's a problem.

If you think that you can just have your retirement party and then magically flip that switch to being a retired person, you may be in for a shock. While many people used to receive a pension check every month that paid for all of their retirement needs, that's usually not an option anymore. It's more complicated than that nowadays.

The vast majority of Americans don't have a pension plan today, just Social Security. What if your pension, even with your Social Security, won't cover all your expenses? You're going to find yourself in an income gap month after month. That means that your money is going to run out eventually. We'll show you strategies designed to provide you with lifetime income.

Even if you never meet us, we're going to offer you the chance to learn more about retirement finances so that you can take control of them. We've put the basics in this book. We think that when you're done reading, you'll still want to consult us. That's up to you. We need to say this: In our opinion, retirement wealth planning is not a do-it-yourself opportunity. Read our book, then consult us with your ideas, goals, and dreams. We'll help you plan to realize them all.

Please keep in mind that there is no one single way to retire. Anyone who tells you there's one best method of retirement planning is selling you something. Don't buy. Say, "Thanks for your time," and find an independent planner. We are independent planners, and we show every client that there are a lot of good options out there, all of them as unique as you are. Your retirement plan should fit you and your loved ones, not be squeezed into some sales-man's cookie-cutter plan. Your money should be safe, not constantly at risk. Your retirement should only impact your quality of life for the better, with your nest egg organized to support you through all the remaining years of your life.

Our goal is for you to live your best retired life and make better financial decisions because you have access to better retirement advice. Let's see how to start on your best foot.

BASIC WAYS RETIREMENT HAS CHANGED FOR US ALL

We'd like to start by giving you a little background. We have both been assisting retirees for long enough to observe changes in how retirement unfolds for Americans. Raymond will talk about that in light of his fifty-year career. You need to read that because your retirement is not like your parents' retirement. Things have changed for almost all retirees, and you can't base your decisions on what your parents did back then.

Chris says, "We find that many new clients are focused on the amount of money they have saved. We know that this is not even remotely the right focus! It's different for everybody, but we talk to clients to discover how they live their lives. Our goal is to help them thrive."

Our first advice to every client is to start with the end in sight—exactly because of how retirement is different today from our parents' or grandparents' retirements.

WE START WITH THE END IN SIGHT

Having this discussion in Chapter 1 may seem like we have "the cart before the horse" to you, but we want to start at the end. In fact, we always do. Every client starts at the end with us and is thankful they did.

What do we mean by "the end"?

That's your estate plan, drafted by an attorney.

Now, before you protest that you aren't the neighborhood billionaire, keep reading. You may discover that you don't know what you don't know about estate plans—until you know it.

Here is one thing you don't know: Writing up your total estate plan is your first step toward a successful retirement.

Your TEP: Total Estate Plan

Now, you might think that we're trying to sell you something more than our usual services here with our talk of estate planning. Actually, we are trying to save you money, time, and heartache. The cost of *not* having these documents in place has the potential to be tens or even hundreds of thousands of dollars. It can take months, or even longer than a year, for a drawn-out probate process to conclude. All that time, your family is grieving you.

There's one sad thing that has not much changed statistically in the United States over the years since Raymond founded his business. According to Caring.com and its 2025 survey, 76 percent of respondents indicated that they don't have a will.[1] When someone dies without a will, it's called *intestate*. Dying intestate leaves heirs and loved ones at a big loss when you pass away. It doesn't need to be that way.

People can get deathly ill at any age. We all know this. If they have no medical power of attorney in place, they might be in trouble when it comes to making serious medical decisions.

People can become disabled at any age. If they have no financial power of attorney in place to manage their money and bills, they might be in trouble.

People can pass away at any age and from just about any cause you can name.

---

1   Victoria Lurie, *2025 Wills and Estate Planning Study*, Caring, updated September 15, 2025, https://www.caring.com/resources/wills-survey#who-has-a-will?.

Don't be like so many Americans who pass without an estate plan.

At Bostian Retirement Planning and Wealth Management", we don't go for that. Not for you. You need a plan. That's why we ask clients to create these documents at our first meeting with them. We offer estate planning support services through strategic partnerships with elder law and estate planning attorneys whom we trust, so our clients can get their estate plan done—and done right. That surely sets us apart from other retirement wealth planners, and our clients notice!

Our clients are often just stunned at the idea of having a total estate plan (TEP). As we hear over and over, "But guys, we aren't billionaires. This is billionaire stuff!" No, it is not. It is "wise man stuff." Our clients are now wise. Educated. All of them stand taller with that estate plan in hand.

In that first appointment with them, our discussion about estate planning is to educate them. They see we are talking with them from 360 degrees—the full picture of who they are, what they need and want, what their goals are. But then? The estate planning attorney, our strategic partner, also gives them legally drafted documents that prove that their estate plan is real.

We offer a complimentary estate strategy planning session to every single one of our clients at our very first appointment with them.

Let's see what exactly it is that we talk about with our clients.

A Total Estate Plan = Protection and Legacy

Most folks who walk through our doors do not have the following documents:

- A power of attorney for financial matters
- A power of attorney for health care or medical matters
- A will
- A trust

We understand your resistance. We do. First, most people think this is for the very wealthy. Second, they don't want to think about their own death. We understand. Who wants to waste their time being anxious about what could happen?

When you come to Bostian Retirement Planning and Wealth Management, we always educate. The education starts with your TEP, your total estate plan. We discuss the general purpose of each document.

The estate planning attorneys that we partner with will then explain the specific benefits for you and your life. These are several of the most qualified estate planning attorneys in North Carolina; they're experts in creating wills, trusts, and powers of attorney.

As we all know (but hate to think about), none of us knows when it's our time to go. If you don't have these four documents in place, you're setting up all the people you love for a difficult and emotional legal process. That legal nightmare happens while your family is still mourning you, too.

A number of people come into the office thinking that all of their assets should go to their kids. Their entire plan is to just scrape by until they die, then gift everything to the next generation.

It's a noble thought, but there are some huge problems. First, you're still a role model to your adult kids. We are parents, and we know that role never goes away. Don't you think they want you to be happy and have everything you need (including money) during retirement? Most kids would rather have their parents be happy and spend their own money than receive a slightly larger bequest.

What's the best gift you can give your children?

Show them how to live a successful life. That includes you living a nice, long retirement and spending your money!

To really take care of your family, you need to take care of yourself. And that includes putting together your estate plan. It is how your children, heirs, and beneficiaries know what your wishes are. Offering them the peace of mind that you're enjoying your life and are self-sufficient is a huge gift to them. To do that, it's essential to know what danger you're avoiding.

There are many issues to address, many transitional risks to avoid, and many loved ones you'd like to honor. This is what an estate plan is for. That is why there are several documents within it.

Most people don't have their assets in the right places, meaning that you (and your heirs) could face a huge tax burden. We'll talk more about that later in this book. Your estate attorney will also speak about that with you.

Now, let's get into what each document of that estate plan is all about.

Last Will and Testament

It is true, our clients are not billionaires. So we make sure to explain to them what the benefits of a living trust are. We give them our brochure on the topic of living trusts and wills.

Why do you need a last will and testament, often just called a will?

This is the Who Gets What document.

A last will and testament goes into effect only after you die. Don't be like most people who die without a will. When they pass, their assets are all locked up and their loved ones are stuck. With no will, you don't get to decide where your money and all your "stuff" go.

Probate

Upon your passing, your heir(s) must still take your will to probate court. Now, most folks have heard of probate, or probate court. Most, however, don't really know what that means.

Probate is a legal proceeding taking place in a court of law. The court makes sure that the will your heirs present is valid—the most recent one. Next, the court's objective is to make sure that your debts are paid. Finally, your assets are distributed according to your will.

That's well and good. So what's the problem with probate?

Plenty!

- If you die without a will or any estate document (intestate), the state you live in will distribute your assets according to the laws they have in place.
- However, even with a valid will when you pass away, heirs do not avoid probate because a will must be verified by the probate court before it can be enforced.
- It's expensive, or it can be. You have legal fees, executor fees, and court costs to pay before your assets are fully distributed to your beneficiaries.
- If your assets are located in different states, you need probate in each state.
- It's time-consuming.
  » Probate court cases can take up to two years to resolve. During that time, all the assets are frozen.
  » That means no one can touch them or access them. Property cannot be sold.
  » If you have beneficiaries who need money to live on, they are stuck. They can't touch yours.

- Contrary to a living trust (see below), which keeps your business private, once you are in probate court, your affairs are public.
  » If all you have left behind is the last will and testament, your heirs will be in probate court.
  » The public aspect of the process may be uncomfortable for some of your beneficiaries.

That is not the end of how a probate process works, but that's the big picture for now. You really want to avoid probate court for your heirs and beneficiaries if you possibly can. And, depending on your situation, you may be able to with a *total* estate plan like our clients create with the estate planning attorneys we partner with.

The next piece is the trust.

Your Living Trust

A living trust is for your financial affairs. It outlines your wishes for the assets held in the trust. What are the benefits of having a living trust?

Contrary to a will, which takes effect upon your death, the living trust is in effect during your lifetime. A living trust is relatively inexpensive to set up and maintain, and if properly structured, it can prevent court control of your assets if you are incapacitated. With a trust, you are assured of certain things:

- Your beneficiaries avoid probate upon your death.
- Your assets are all brought together into one plan.
- Your business, your assets, and your wealth are private matters.
- You can ensure quicker distribution of your assets and bequests to your heirs and beneficiaries.
- Your assets can remain in the trust until you want beneficiaries to inherit them. In other words, you can state in your trust document when and how your assets are distributed.
- You can change your living trust or even cancel it as you wish.[2]
- A professionally drafted living trust is very difficult to contest.
- You can prevent unintentional disinheritance or other problems of joint ownership.
- You can get professional management with a corporate trustee (or the trustee could be a family member or other trusted individual).

We explain the benefits and differences between a living trust and a last will, and why you can benefit from having both.

---

2   The ability to change or revoke a trust is not always possible depending on the type of trust. Please seek guidance from a qualified estate planning attorney.

And last but not least? You have peace of mind that you have stated your wishes. They are documented, legally. You have taken care of your loved ones in the process.

You are not yet done, however.

Powers of Attorney

A trust is not the same as a will. Your two powers of attorney likewise serve very different, additional functions for you.

Why is a will not enough? Your assets are not protected with just the will if you become physically or mentally incapacitated. In the case of incapacity, the courts could easily take control of your assets before you die. You can change that with the following powers of attorney (POA).

1. The financial power of attorney (financial POA)

It names one or more trusted individuals who will manage your financial affairs and make financial decisions for you if you are incapacitated and cannot do this yourself.

This POA is for managing assets and business matters outside the trust. Think about monthly bill payments and that sort of thing.

2. The medical power of attorney (health care POA)

It names one or more trusted individuals who will manage your medical and health care affairs. They make medical decisions for you if you are incapacitated and cannot do this yourself. You might develop Alzheimer's or another illness or condition, making you unable to understand and decide about all the types of medical needs you have on your own.

So you see how the four documents—your TEP—are both designed for protection and legacy.

What Is Our SWAN Cure?

We've had many clients in the past who came in to set up a retirement portfolio. That's all they *thought* they needed to do. We set them straight. They took advantage of our complementary estate strategy planning session and sat down with an estate attorney whom we trust and recommend.

An estate plan is not about your retirement per se. How so? Some of our TEP and retirement planning clients have passed away before they even retired. Having a TEP meant that the transfer of their assets to protect their spouses was smooth and seamless. For them, as for you, estate planning instructs your heirs about what happens upon your passing. They did the right thing. Even if they didn't get to live out the retirement they expected to, their families were taken care of.

Do you see why we want to "start with the end in sight" and set up your TEP? The right thing for you to do is also the right thing for your family. We can't stress that enough. That's why we focus on your TEP first. If you don't have a clear end to a plan, then it's not really a plan at all.

Here's the best part of just getting it out of the way, even if it's uncomfortable. When you've already processed all those difficult topics and written up what your wishes are, you sleep better!

You won't have to constantly think about those "what if" scenarios because they're all accounted for. Your plan is in place. You can just enjoy the peace of mind of spending however many years you have left living out that plan and enjoying your retirement.

We call this the SWAN cure: *Sleep Well At Night.* Because your estate plan is in place and properly documented, you sleep well. No worries. No what-ifs left unanswered.

Communication

Your remaining job is to communicate with those you trust. Tell them:

1. you have estate planning documents,
2. where they are located or who holds them, and
3. the POA you have named has agreed to
   be your POA.

This last point is so important that we have to tell you a story.

Not long ago, we spoke on the phone with a gentleman whose mother started working with Raymond way back before Chris joined the business. The gentleman's mother passed away last year when she was ninety. At the time of her death, he turned to a tax attorney and two different financial advisors he already knew about how to access his mother's bequests. He didn't think to come to us right away, for some reason.

Anyway, those professionals were unable to answer the questions he had, which were questions we answer every day. And boy, did he have questions! He needed to know about her life insurance policy, IRA, non-IRA brokerage account, several non-IRA annuities, and where the heck her last will was. None of those other professionals knew how to track the paperwork or advise him in any way.

Well, it finally occurred to her son to get in touch with us. He finally remembered that we were her retirement planners!

When we answered each of his questions clearly and instantly, he was amazed. We just told him, "We know your mom created her TEP with our strategic-partner estate attorney. We know about your mother's financial investments because Chris was her portfolio advisor. We know your mother's tax picture. We also know how to get you the release of bequests you need. It's what we do."

Then we reassured him. We sensed that he thought we would be trying to sell him something. Nothing was further from the truth. We just told him, "You can move the money wherever you want to. It is yours now."

He won't need probate or a court order to access his late parent's estate, as he believed he did. We could tell him when his mom's money would be ready to be released.

He was so relieved at how easy having an estate plan made things!

Here is another aspect of the TEP: We had already explained all those bequest and beneficiary issues to his mother. She understood. However, she clearly didn't turn around and explain her money and legacy arrangements to her heirs or loved ones.

Now we always make sure that we—and the estate attorneys we partner with—gently remind our clients that *they don't need to reveal all their secrets to their beneficiaries.* They should, however, tell their beneficiaries and their heirs *where* to find the answers they need when the time comes.

Draw up your total estate plan. Then share with your loved ones at least where to find the documents and how to proceed.

We educate each client on how to do that. Know this: You never need to reveal the Who Gets What to your beneficiaries if you don't want to. But those heirs do need to know how to access the Who Gets What when you pass.

You deserve better than people who pass away intestate. They're leaving their beneficiaries and heirs to figure out the mess. Don't leave a mess. Leave a legacy.

CHAPTER 2

RAYMOND'S REFLECTIONS ON FIFTY YEARS

We are soon marking an important occasion. In January 2026, the Bostian Retirement Planning and Wealth Management firm is entering its fiftieth year of service to retirees. We decided to mark the event with this book. We'll also host an all-clients-welcome event in early 2026.

Because I founded the company, Chris has comically deferred to me to reminisce about my years in the business. He said I'm allowed to have a whole chapter to ramble, so here I go.

When people walk into our office, our receptionist greets them. They're offered a dessert and a drink while they're waiting for their meeting. Also, we let people coming to meet with us know that there is no charge for a consultation with us.

On the left wall in the reception area is a big picture of our staff with a Christian inscription.

Those things haven't changed over the years we have been in business. We just want to let people who come to us know that they are welcome and they can feel relaxed about talking with us.

Learning the Business

When I opened the doors to my business on September 6, 1976, I knew nothing about retirement planning. Oh, boy, has that changed!

My four years of college were in business management, but I knew nothing about retirement planning. And, of course, I was fresh out of college, so I was not looking to plan my own retirement right then either!

I took a job right out of college with a company that was a leader in this industry and offered the top programs for retirement. They educated me—they taught me a lot.

Since my very first client appointment, there's been one big way that retirement has changed for retirees. There's also been one big way that it has not changed at all.

Big Change for Retirees

My dad worked at a factory pretty much his whole career. Most people of his generation in retirement were like him. They got a pat on the back, a handshake from the company president, a gold watch, and a pension. I have to say, my dad didn't even get a gold watch. He got a pension from the textile factory. He retired with that pension and his Social Security—like many retirees I advised in those early days.

Can you name anyone earning a pension nowadays? It has become very rare. So that's the first change in our retirement outlook.

People still had pensions in my early years in this business. Their pension was actually an *annuity*, though most people didn't think of it that way. It was guaranteed to them for life. They would add their Social Security, which was also guaranteed to them for life (as it is today). Those two mailbox paychecks, as I like to call them, were their retirement money for the most part back then. Nobody worried much beyond that, because their two sources of income in retirement were guaranteed for life.

My staff says I coined the term *mailbox paycheck*. Back then, people got their money by check in the mail. That's where I got that. I called the guaranteed-for-life income their mailbox money or their mailbox paycheck. I still use the term, and people like it. It lands in their account every month, guaranteed.

What I learned right away, fifty years ago, was about annuities beyond just Social Security and pensions. Annuities had been well known for over a century by then. Twenty years into my career, there was one more change. In the 1990s, annuities went mainstream. They were no longer some corporation's or those well-heeled clients' secret. They evolved into a **very** important additional source of retirement income, as we'll discuss in a later chapter.

So why do I talk about change here? Employers were starting to do away with the pensions. They decided it was too costly for the company. Plus, managing and safeguarding that money for decades was a burden on them that wasn't aligned with their real line of work.

What came in to replace the pension was the 401(k) retirement account. You, the employee, put money in it—money you had not yet paid income tax on—and saved and saved.

I've been a retirement specialist through both eras. The 401(k) has some pluses and some minuses.

The Good

The great plus is that companies payroll-deduct that money for a 401(k) qualified account. The employee says, "Take this much," and it's automated. Without that automation, most people just wouldn't save for retirement in that 401(k). Employers can leave the pensions behind and still offer a kind of retirement savings solution to their employees.

Another plus is that employers may also provide a match that could be up to a percentage or dollar amount. The contributions I've seen are typically around 6 percent of your income, but you'll want to check with your employer to see what their match is. That gives people the incentive to save even more money into that 401(k). After all, who doesn't want "free money" from their employer?

One more plus is that the employee has less taxable income that year by putting pre-taxed money in the account. Everyone is happy to think about the tax burden later.

Now, here are the minuses.

The Bad

With pensions, the money just came out of your paycheck before you touched it. You had no choice about it. You paid in. That was that.

For a 401(k), you are on your own to say, "Yes, I'm in. I'm putting in X percent of my paycheck every pay period." You decide whether to participate or not. You have to figure out how much (up to the legal limit). That was the first difference for retirees.

You also suddenly—with no education about how the financial industry or investing worked—have an "investment" account. Money in a 401(k) account is largely invested in the markets, but not only there. On top of that, you probably don't know how it is being invested on your behalf. Is it *wisely* invested? You certainly never know that.

That is a huge negative point for almost everyone. You have to understand this: Going into retirement, you need a *retirement* plan, not an *investment* plan.

A 401(k) is not a pension. It is not a mailbox paycheck. It was never designed for that. It was really designed so the companies could get away from managing those pensions for decades. That meant an employee ended up not with a guaranteed monthly payout straight from their employer's pension fund, but with a lump sum of money in their own account. Now what?

This evolution to self-management hurt people, in my opinion. They were getting toward retirement, and they didn't know how to manage that pot of 401(k) money. They had no education about the market risk I mentioned. That's a big, big downside of the 401(k). It's just a pot of money that you have to figure out how to turn into retirement income.

As my training and experience progressed in the business, I saw that I could never have taken a course in college that taught me anything about helping people manage their retirement. Those kinds of classes didn't exist, of course. I saw really quickly that retirement was something that you didn't learn in a book. I learned it through hands-on experience on the job and from the guidance I got at that first company.

Even if I had been able to learn this in college, times change quickly.

And speaking of education, I told you there was one big thing that has not changed in my fifty years in this business.

Be the Educator

The one thing that the first company I was with told me was, "Raymond, most people don't know what they don't know until they know. That's why you have to educate them on retirement. When the day starts or the day ends, you're going to be a *retirement planning educator.* That means that you've got to use your good education, sure. But you've also got to use your good, God-given common sense. You're going to gain a lot of experience with retirees. The first thing you'll learn is just that most retirees do not know anything about retirement."

I saw that it was true, right from the start. I did see it. People didn't know what they needed to know. That has not changed.

Then my company trainer told me, "A person will come to us thinking that retirement is working one day and quitting work so that the next day they're in retirement and they don't have to worry about a thing."

That picture retirees had in their heads was far from the truth, as I quickly discovered.

My trainers were correct. Retirees back then had to worry about getting their pension in place and had very little information on how to do that to their best advantage. They didn't know much about getting Medicare started. The ones with retirement accounts—IRAs, and those early 401(k) and 403(b) accounts—didn't know how they should spend that pot of money to make it last.

Nobody, but nobody, understood their future tax picture at all. That was a big, black hole for everyone.

I also heard, "Raymond, one spouse dies first. Count on it. But the surviving spouse is going to have a lot of problems that you can help eliminate. Let them know right away that they can come to you and pour out their questions." We have done that from our earliest days. We usually have great answers for the surviving spouse's many questions.

People didn't know what to do to make sure the right beneficiaries received their assets when they passed away (and you know my solution to that from Chapter 1).

From my earliest days operating my own company, I have observed this to be true: Most retirees who are "getting ready" for that transition from one day working to being retired the next day have not received the retirement planning education they need. They didn't know they needed it! They are not really ready. That remains true today.

We educate every single client with the goal of helping them rest easy in their retirement.

They never ask, "Now why did Raymond or Chris make that one change for me?" They know why, because we walk them through every new document, every change to their plan, every reorganization of their finances. They don't get to walk out until they understand!

Those trainers of mine told me that I was going to learn really quickly that to be successful at helping people entering or in retirement was to tell them, "I'm going to be here for years and decades. This is my profession. You can come in and talk when you have worries . . . because you're family." That's what I do to this day. Clients are family.

Independent Financial Professionals

In those early days, I also learned something really beneficial for all our clients. In my training, I learned an important fact about many retirement planners, financial advisors, bank brokers, and insurance agents. They just sell the products their employer recommends that they sell.

We don't do that. From the start, I created us to be independent of any one "product" company. We look at a wide variety of financial products on the US market for our clients, so we always have options to meet our client's unique needs and goals. We're not locked in.

We don't only sell products. We also sell service. We provide education. That means both of us provide answers (or the attorneys we partner with do). By providing service, we are also providing education to every single client. We don't just do a thing for them and say, "See you next year." We explain not just what they need but also show them the options out there to address their needs. We listen to what they want. We present options for being able to get that, too. We explain how the strategy works for them. We can't do that unless we listen. We want to hear them from a 360-degree perspective.

Client Involvement

Now, talking about your money can be emotional. You don't want anyone telling you that you're a bad money manager. Some people hate to reveal how they spend their money.

They hate for anyone to tell them they're wrong. But we need lots of information if we're going to help you retire successfully, and that means knowing all about your money, certainly. We also get familiar with your goals, your needs, and your wants. We let you talk about your family with us. It gives us the best picture to create your best retirement plan.

My trainers back then told me, "Raymond, you've got to learn the magic words in your sales service and life career. And those words are always saying, 'Yes, sir. Yes, ma'am. No, sir. No, ma'am. Please. Thank you.' Then let the client know *you need their help*."

What did my trainer mean? That's a magic statement you make to a client. "I need your help. Will you help me?" They'll always come back with, "Oh! What do you need help with, Mr. Bostian?" Then I say, "I need to get some input from you. I need some information to show you the problems that exist that you're not even aware of. When you see the problems, we can find solutions together."

My trainer was 100 percent right. I learned that when I started asking these questions, it evolved really quickly. Those simple words established a partnership with new clients.

Other advisors might just talk at you, not with you. They may not be good listeners. They may not ask you many questions, or at least not the right ones.

People don't care how much you know about *your product* until they know how much you care about *them*. Getting them involved in their own solution was the purpose of that

"I need your help" statement. Getting their information to provide them with solutions and education got them involved in making the right decision for themselves.

People need to be able to relate to you. They like to see the proof that you know what you're talking about. That you're not judging them. That you're helping them. I think we achieve that for our clients.

Our educational approach—our participation approach—helps people feel more in control of their money and their future security.

In addition to asking my clients to help me and participate in their own retirement planning, I was trained to use a checklist of about a dozen or so things to make sure that on the day they transition into retirement, they have all of the paperwork completed, all of their beneficiaries are named and filed, and all of their i's are dotted and t's are crossed.

The result of this care is, hopefully, that our newest and our oldest clients trust us to educate them in their favor. To be acting in their best interest (and not ours). To inform them in plenty of time when a change might be coming up. We tell clients what might happen so it doesn't happen.

That's what our team calls providing education and service.

When you're in a service profession, the lack of attention to a client will lose you that client. People will leave their other advisor, not because of a lack of returns or lack of product choices. They'll leave because of that advisor's lack of care, lack of service, and lack of teaching them. They'll leave due to the lack of contact with the advisor.

I can state this, hand on my heart, because over my whole fifty years, I have heard, "Oh, Mr. Bostian! I needed someone who *listened*. I needed someone who *explained* where my money was and why. My old advisor wasn't doing that. I was *that* nervous! I just closed out everything over there and came to you, like my neighbor So-and-So told me. So-and-So said he's been with you for years, and you *explain everything!*"

And we do. That's the kind of reference we love and work for—yes, indeed.

I transitioned quickly in the first few years from being an insurance-product representative to being, more accurately, a retirement educator. I consider Chris and myself to be outstanding educators. We tell clients what's going to happen before it happens. If the new client comes in without a good retirement plan, we say so, or if they come in with a risky investment plan, Chris will show them why it's risky. If the client does not know anything about how they can make it safe, we show and explain that to them. If they don't have their beneficiaries correctly designated, or none are named at all, we take care to explain why that is so important to correct.

In other words, we take care of the urgent items first, but we don't rush. We take the time to explain all along the way what needs to be taken care of first, how, and why. We don't do anything for a client that they 1) don't understand or 2) don't agree with. We serve their goals. Not ours. We are the educators. They are the decision-makers.

Stories Educate

I guess I'm just a storyteller. I use stories to explain concepts to people. Storytelling is my approach to education, so people can relate their lives to the retirement plan we're setting up.

I don't act like a salesperson at all. I don't "tell them" and expect them to trust anything I've said. I make a story out of it. I give them plenty of real examples.

Statements tell, stories sell.

That's what we do. That's it.

The Top Five: From Fearful to Fearless

I want to give you just a word in general about risk. We will address this big topic in several chapters. There are types of risk that we will discuss in some detail because most people don't know what risk they're going to have until it hits them crossways.

One thing that I learned early on in my work is that *everyone's* transition into retirement holds risks that people don't see coming. Nowadays, people are living longer than they did fifty years ago. They are retiring earlier than our parents did. The longer somebody lives, the more likely they're going to have all kinds of risks associated with that longer life—unless they plan for it.

Another aspect of my work with clients that hasn't changed is that people get scared when we talk about the worst problems that they could have. Here are the top five scary topics that I have seen over all my years doing this work.

Mention that the wrong person might inherit their money and other treasures when they pass away, and they're scared. That's why your total estate plan from Chapter 1 is the topic of our first appointment together with every client. We resolve that fear. They decide Who Gets What, document it, and the fear goes away.

Mention a bear market, and they get worried. They know their 401(k) or IRA money is in the stock market. They're scared to death of the market, and they're scared of losing it all. Chris provides portfolio management services because we know our clients cannot do that planning on their own. Chris explains how reorganization of their portfolio helps to address their worries.

Mention they could potentially live past a hundred, and their face says it all! Shock. Concern. Worry. Right now and in the recent past, we have had clients in their hundred-plus years. This is not theoretical or statistical. It's real life today.

Now, if you retire in your sixties or even in your seventies, *that's a retirement lasting as long as your working years did!* That fear of outliving your money is still real. What will you do if, say, at age eighty-nine, your money is gone? If that other advisor used that "average American life expectancy" statistic to figure out how long your money needs to last—well, you're in hot water as a centenarian. Rest assured, my team and I don't think (or calculate) like that! We'll discuss this possibility with you and how you can make sure you have lifetime income.[3]

Mention just plain running out of money at any age after retirement, and they get worried. Overspending—or spending without a plan and running out of money—is the stuff of nightmares for a lot of people. That's why we talk about both an income plan and a spending plan, so that the two plans match up. We'll talk about how we do this in a later chapter.

Mention owing big money to Uncle Sam during retirement, and people break out in a sweat. They fear not having the money to settle their taxes. It is possible to manage it. You do have to plan. We walk through the solutions that exist, and our clients calm down and breathe more easily.

Let me just say here and now that our clients are all very grateful that we've opened their eyes to risks that exist. Otherwise, they would have been blindsided. We tell them that we also have solutions to reduce or eliminate those potential or real risks. As one client said, "First, you scared me. Then you calmed me down."

That's our job. We educate you about what might happen. We give you knowledge. We let you make decisions

---

3   Lifetime income guarantees are backed by the financial strength and
      claims-paying ability of the issuing insurance company.

based on knowledge. Then we give you ways to help prevent the bad things from happening whenever possible.

I can't overstate the relief our clients feel when we resolve or reduce these risks to their money. They need us to tell them, "No, it's just education. We'll teach you. We'll reorganize your money in ways that benefit you and that you understand. Then you'll be able to live out your retirement knowing you have a plan to address these risks. We'll put solutions in place."

Common Sense Is So Uncommon

Retirement success, in my opinion, is an 80/20 proposition. It's 80 percent common sense and 20 percent book sense. What happens if you lose a lot of money in retirement? You're going to have a worse retirement. That's common sense.

Now, some believe their money has to be in the stock market. They dream of doubling their money. But I ask them, "If you doubled your money, would that change your lifestyle? Probably not. You'd still eat the same amount of food at the same restaurants. You'd still go on the same trips. Your clothes would be about what they are now. But if doubling your money won't change you, think about losing 50 percent of your money. Would that change you and how you live? Yes, absolutely. Of course, it would." So, if doubling your money wouldn't change your circumstances much, while losing half of your money would, doesn't it make more common sense to have a safe retirement plan to help eliminate losing big in retirement?

Other people (and we'll tell you those stories) are so tight with their money, it is amazing it's not just all tucked under their mattress while they live (as Grandad would have said) on toothpicks and water. So I ask these folks, "Do you know that your money could have earned X more dollars if you'd done this other thing instead? Do you know there is still time to grow?"

Fear and risk are wound up in each other. Education can show you ways to address fear and risk.

Safe-Money Professionals

That leads me to one other thing that sets us apart. We come from a safe-money mentality. We use all types of calculators, software tools, strategies, and products to offer a large blend of guaranteed retirement income products while Chris can help you invest some of your money to combat inflation in later years.

We like our independent status. Having a full range of products and solutions that are on the American market is a huge benefit to our clients. We're able to do that because we're independent advisors.

In our office, Chris is a fiduciary, which means that (because of his role as an investment advisor representative) he is legally required to always act in each client's best interest. Our commitment is that everyone else in our office also act as fiduciaries, even in the absence of a legal requirement. I think that's a big thing with the evolution of our industry, too—there are many "financial service professionals" but not enough "fiduciaries," so we have chosen to work in our clients' best interests.

We see it as our job to help you keep your retirement money as safe as possible while giving you the income you need. We call this a safe-money strategy. Annuities—especially fixed indexed annuities—help us keep your money safe. (I could talk all day about that topic, but I'll leave it to a later chapter.)

To sum up what has *not changed* in our business over the decades:

- We are educators.
- We are independent.
- We get our clients to participate in the process for a successful retirement.
- We know how to set you up with a retirement "mailbox paycheck."

Chris and I, along with our whole staff, have worked hard, first to learn and then to share the right knowledge with our clients.

We never impose a retirement plan on any client. We educate them about their money, what the risks are, and how they could keep their money safer. That education is the only way they can make informed decisions. We've found that they start sleeping better at night without their fears and worries eating away at them. They come to see us at no additional charge. Every time they have a life change, they call on us to document it and to ask if the life change affects their financial picture. We discuss it and present options. We make the needed adjustments.

That's why I say that it has been very rare for us to sit with somebody in a first, exploratory meeting who doesn't become a client. They get big relief because we're educating them. We don't hold back. We tell people how their money might be at risk. Then we tell them how they can keep it safer. We create strategies to reduce or potentially even eliminate some risks to their retirement money.

We spend time getting to know our clients from a 360-degree perspective. This has led to a very pleasant evolution, indeed. Today, 100 percent of our clients come to us as referrals. New clients are referred to us by current clients now. Our current clients brag about how we've set them up with lifetime income. They brag about how we educate them. Their friends and other family want some of that.

We don't feel like we have any competition. Banks, brokers, insurance companies, agents—they're not competition to us because they're not taking the time to teach their clients, to listen to them, to pull them into their family.

Your Hard Work Should Pay Off

I have worked hard for fifty years. I grew up on a farm, working hard for ten- to sixteen-hour days when I was a little bitty thing, and I learned a good work ethic.

I tell everybody that I don't think anybody outworked me. I might not be the smartest person, but I've got a good college education and a lot of God-given common sense. My work ethic is still sound and solid after all this time.

Here's what I already understand about you: You, too, have worked hard all your life. You saved. You put money away. You wanted to be independent in your later years. You worked toward retirement.

I believe your lifetime of hard work should pay off.

I'm going to work hard to help educate you so you understand your money and your arrangements. I'll help you plan for a safe, financially successful retirement. I know you've been working toward it all your life.

I want to make you part of the Bostian Retirement family. That's my goal.

People Don't Change Much

In the end, as I look back, I think people still want what they want. Over decades, they have established their lifetime habits, their values, goals, and interests. That's always going to be the same.

Like they say: "Times change. Values don't."

I've always joked that people don't really change. A zebra doesn't change its stripes. I think people adapt to what's going on and just keep on going. That fact leads us to also joke "once a saver, always a saver" because that is one of their habits. If you have somebody open and curious to look outside of what they've always done, I think they're always going to have that curiosity. People don't change; they just adapt themselves or adapt their plan to what's going on.

That's the whole point of what we're trying to get across to people when we discuss how their lives are going to be different once they make that transition into retirement. We say, "You have to be ready. Sometimes you won't always be able to do what you've always done. What you do with our help and experience is adapt in a way that still suits you."

My half-century of working with people to prepare their most successful retirement has proved it to me: I believe every retiree needs to be involved with a retirement planner or an advisor who has a solutions mentality, a curiosity.

This book is called *The Basics of Retirement* for a reason. There are some essential ingredients in a successful retirement. These are your basics—the necessities. We have spoken about your total estate plan. I've reminisced a bit (and rambled quite a lot!) about my fifty years as a retirement income planner. Now let me join Chris again and get into the remaining essential ingredients of your retirement plan. As you'll see, I've already hinted at a number of them.

CHAPTER 3

GETTING TO KNOW YOU

Everything we do every day at Bostian Retirement Planning and Wealth Management is designed to create one outcome: all of our clients will have the most successful retirement possible. When our clients are experiencing success during their retirement, that's a success we share. It's what keeps us going.

We treat our clients like family. As you detected from our Chapter 1 discussion of your TEP, or total estate plan, we do have a process that we use when we meet with our clients.

That process is designed to fulfill our dual mission, which is to:

1. Protect and preserve your nest egg from loss and risks, where possible.
2. Ensure that you have a sufficient income throughout your life.

Our process involves having in-depth conversations with you (always confidential) from a 360-degree angle. What we mean by 360 degrees is that we like to know the full circle—more than just your financial situation and your financial goals. Of course, we do ask you to bring in your most recent financial statements, banking statements, trading account statements, and so on. However, you are more than your money! Retirement is about much more than money.

We will also ask you about your retirement goals. We want to hear all those wonderful (and sometimes crazy!) items on your Big Deal Bucket List. You should feel at ease telling us your worries and your fears so that we can help create a retirement plan designed specifically for you.

It's true. Lots of new clients think we start right away by crunching the numbers. They think all we do is look at how much wealth you have and where it is invested, and so on. Sure, we do that, yes, indeed. But we do it *second*.

You have seen that we start with your TEP. Then we will continue with you to discuss your total financial retirement plan.

You Are in the Driver's Seat

We want to state something here, and state it quite clearly: We do not make any financial decisions for you. That is not our role. That is not how we work with you or for you.

We also like all of our clients to also understand this quite clearly: There is no such thing as being risk-free when it comes to money.

For a successful retirement, our key focus with you is *eliminating, when legitimately possible,* as many of the risks to your money as possible. When we cannot eliminate, we proceed to *reduce* the remaining risks to the degree we can. (We'll be discussing risks and how to eliminate or reduce them in several chapters of this book, so stick around.)

We are retirement income planners. As such, we strive to do three things quite well for all our clients.

1. Education

We educate you about the risks to your money in retirement. This is not to scare you, but to help you understand what the various risks are. In our experience, most people never identify all of them. We attempt to. You can come in as often as you need to (at no additional charge) to talk through and get clear on any aspect of your retirement plan you want. Once you understand the concepts, we present the options you have available to reduce risk and Chris can present options to reorganize your finances. Then we ask you to decide what you want to do based on your new knowledge.

2. Risk Reduction

We reduce (and eliminate, where possible) the risks to your money according to your wishes and decisions about it—not ours. We present financial and other instruments to achieve this. We discuss ways to reorganize your money to achieve this reduction in risk. But again, once we have educated you about them, it's up to you what actions you take.

3. Predictable, Guaranteed Retirement Income

We help you create a guaranteed stream of retirement income that covers or exceeds your spending needs in retirement.

If that or anything we've said so far seems like a promise we can't fulfill, keep reading. We're not blowing smoke.

Other financial services professionals may not ask you many questions. They might look primarily at your money, not your life or your goals. They might give you a cookie-cutter plan; they may even invest your money according to their corporation's cookie-cutter products.

We don't do that. Your plan will be custom-tailored to you only.

Now, one last thing. Creating a whole book may seem like a lot to just present "the basics" of retirement. But in our long experience, all of this information is necessary for you to plan for the most successful, worry-free retirement you can.

You see, people just don't know what they don't know—until they finally know it.

That's what we're all about. We give you the information you need to help you achieve a retirement that's happy and matched to your financial needs.

CHAPTER 4

ONE TIP FOR A GREAT RETIREMENT

While this aspect of your life is not an "official" part of our retirement wealth planning with you, our long, shared experience leads us to make a few comments anyway.

It comes down to this:

Without your health, no amount of cash savings, successful investments, or beautiful possessions matters. No amount of financial planning matters.

However, with a strong body, mind, and spirit, you can accomplish just about anything you choose. To us, this is just common sense (and you know what the skeptics say about *that*).

At Any Age

The Dalai Lama turned ninety years old in 2025, and he has expressed the belief that he can live to the age of 130! He walks daily on a treadmill if he can't be outdoors. He has that positive outlook one expects from this man, but he's also a very good role model about never being too old to treat one's body with respect.

Many readers are familiar with the actor Dick Van Dyke. He celebrated his one-hundredth birthday in December 2025.

We older ones remember with fondness Van Dyke's black-and-white TV show with Mary Tyler Moore. And what about his very successful film, *Mary Poppins*, with Julie Andrews? Then he had a TV hit called *Diagnosis: Murder*, in which he was the lead actor when he was between sixty-eight and seventy-six years of age. That is an age when many folks are in retirement, and yet this man has performed in even more films and TV shows since then.

Here's what Van Dyke says about health and such matters:

"In my 30s, I exercised to look good.

In my 50s, to stay fit.

In my 70s, to stay ambulatory.

In my 80s, to avoid assisted living.

Now, in my 90s, I'm just doing it out of pure defiance."[4]

Van Dyke exercises daily. He puts in three days a week at the gym doing stretching, weights, yoga, and even dancing between machines. He swims laps. And above all, he

---

4   Eddie McKenna, "Are You Built to Move?," *San Pedro Today*, published September 28, 2023, https://sanpedrotoday.com/2023/09/28/are-you-built-to-move/

keeps an optimistic mindset, which he believes contributes to his longevity and well-being, even at this amazing age.

Now, we are not going to talk about another aspect of health in retirement, which is health care insurance—it's a whole book on its own! We are leaving that whole topic for another day.

However, we do want to say a few words about self-care. We feel that we are a common-sense bunch. A lot of caring for your own health at any time in life is just about common sense.

As we observe our clients and talk to them about their personal common-sense approach, we have found that our healthiest, happiest clients do these five common-sense things:

1. They are not couch potatoes! They stay physically active. They get outdoors. They walk. They stretch. They get to the gym. They exercise regularly.

2. They eat right. They eat Mother Nature's good food. They cook from scratch at home most of the time. They keep it light.

3. They stay socially involved. They meet with friends. They are connected with their family. Many have a church community. Others have a volunteer community. They have hobbies that challenge their brains, and they often share them with others.

4. They get their preventive health care, whether lab work or other regular exams. We have to say that health insurance of most kinds favors this type of exam, and it's encouraged, mostly with no copay.

5. They have, for the most part, a positive mental outlook. They are optimistic about mankind. They are generally compassionate individuals.

This is all common-sense self-care.

We try to practice what we preach, as they say. We're family men. Chris likes to spend time reading, hiking, spending time at the lake with family, and swimming. Raymond hunts and is a fisherman. It gets us out in the world, into nature, and just lets us take a deep breath after a busy work week.

Now, are you going to have some bumps in the road, health-wise, throughout the years? Sure. Isn't that part of just living your life? We will all get that heavy chest cold, that flu. It passes. We might break a bone at some point in our lives. It heals. We might suffer an injury and need to work hard with physical therapy to get our strength and stamina back.

Just look at those things as bumps in the road as you continue to build and maintain your overall good health and wellness. Common sense, right?

We have retiree clients of all ages. And you know that we like to talk about the Go-Go years (the first ten to fifteen years or so of your retirement), the Slow-Go years (the next ten years or so), and the No-Go years (all your remaining years). But as Dick Van Dyke pointed out to us, even in those later years—when you are in your nineties and approaching your centennial birthday—you can take care of your mind's and your body's health.

Let's face it. We work hard for our money for forty or more years. But money is useless to us without our health. The medical industry is a necessity, but it should not be our crutch. We need to make wise choices all the years of our lives and do the best we can with what we've got.

Health can be preserved and enhanced at any age, and it's a fact that our elder population is making meaningful progress in this area. We have better information today because of highly credible professionals sharing it on the internet. There is just no excuse for us today to say, "Well, I don't know what to do." Find out!

We believe that staying healthy for life will help you maximize your enjoyment during your retirement years. Try those top five tips above so that we see you in our offices in tip-top form year after year!

PART TWO

THE BASICS OF WORKING WITH RETIREMENT PLANNING PROFESSIONALS

The reason our business now enjoys a 100 percent referral rate for new clients is pretty straightforward. We've worked toward this outcome for many years.

We strive to be the only independent retirement income planning team that any retiree could ever need.

Second, we're in this field because we love people. We care about people. We love to share our knowledge so that people we advise are even more successful than they dreamed.

Chris says, "Our approach is not to focus on your life's savings, even though that is what you were doing all those years before retirement. We focus on your life's work—preserving it and making your life's work work for you for the rest of your life."

Let's look at what makes a planning professional the right one for you—and when to say "thanks for your time" to the wrong professional and leave the meeting.

CHAPTER 5

OUR BACKGROUND AND APPROACH

Raymond told you about how he started in this field. Chris has been with the business for many years as well. Both of us have intensive training, certifications, and licenses under our belts.

It's all the names the financial industry uses for their certifications and such that make things confusing to the average American looking for qualified professional advice. There are differences in credentials, standards, and compensation structures among professionals who call themselves retirement planners or financial advisors. Practitioners in the retirement planning field use different titles and all sorts of "alphabet soup" designations after their names. Most people have never heard of any of that and usually don't understand what they mean.

You need to know that among all those in this field, education, certification, licensing rigor, and ethical standards differ—and often quite a lot.

When the dust settles, you'll know this: Investment advisor representatives, like Chris, are fiduciaries. This means they are not only ethically but also legally obliged to act in the client's best interest—in *your* best interest.

Too many "planners" out there come into your meeting with a slim folder in their hands. They have barely said hello to you before they open their folder and say, "I've got just the thing right here for you. You need this." No, no, no! That just means they're selling something to you. Thank them and walk out of that meeting! They are keeping their interest up front, not yours.

We actually sit down and talk to our clients. We have conversations. We discuss things back and forth. If the planner you're sitting with right now doesn't do that (or doesn't do that for no additional fee, anytime of the year), say thank you and walk out of that meeting.

A true retirement planner will be interested in YOU, not in selling their corporation's product. And that leads us to say this: We are independent.

We are not locked into any corporate relationship that forces us to sell only one kind of product and just that corporation's product. Here's an easy-to-understand example of home insurance. If you go to a captive insurance agent with XYZ Insurance Company office down the street for homeowners insurance, the agent is obliged to sell you an

XYZ insurance policy. That's it. You would never expect that agent to present an ABC Insurance Company policy! The XYZ agent has no independence to look at the whole market for you; they're locked into XYZ insurance products.

We are not locked in. We are independent of such relationships. We are not under any contract to sell for any corporations. We listen to you and present options from across the industry for you to choose from. We don't do cookie-cutter plans. Chris is securities licensed as an investment advisor representative, and that means he is a fiduciary. Raymond holds himself to that same ethical practice by choice.

What We Do Differently

Under Raymond Bostian's leadership, we started changing lives a long time ago. We've been using the same process since 1976 because it works, it's honest, and it puts you first. People love us for that. It's why they refer their family and friends to us. It's why they talk about us to their children, and then their children end up using our services too.

More recently, with the addition of Wingler Wealth Management, Chris is continuing this tradition for our clients by assisting them with investment advisory services.

We set out on a mission to help people create and grow—and especially keep—their wealth. Our goal is to protect and preserve your hard-earned assets so that you can maximize your life savings.

In the next chapters, we will show you how we do the "keep your wealth" part of retirement planning. We help you reduce your taxes and make sure your retirement portfolio is specifically designed to address your goals with consideration for your risk tolerance.

We set up your total estate plan (TEP), your spending plan, an income plan, and a tax plan so that you can reduce how much of your portfolio you lose to taxes.

We have strategic alliances with top professionals. First are the CPAs, who can help you look forward into your future income and potential tax picture and plan the best way to reduce or eliminate taxes *for your lifetime.* Then there are the estate attorneys, who can discuss your assets, your needs, goals, and wishes, and professionally draft your TEP.

We are trained and continuously educated in our field. We're trained to help you shift your portfolio from financially risky to financially secure.

This approach is all because we have a safe-money mindset—a goal of risk reduction—and will always share strategies with that in mind.

A Successful Retirement

It's our job to set you up for success, no matter what your income or liabilities are when you come to us. You don't have to do retirement planning by yourself. In fact, we say, "Don't DIY this!" In our country, just speak the word "money" and you enter into a whole complicated world where it is too easy to make mistakes. There's too much static out there with so-called professionals puffing up their chests and offering terrible advice (so beware what you hear on social media).

If you're the type of DIY person who wants more hands-on control, we will offer you a true partnership. It will start with us sharing our knowledge with you, because without a financial education, you are likely to make more mistakes. Some of them will be unforgiving! For those who want it done for you, we offer full transparency so that you stay informed about your plan.

A married couple from our town had been valued clients of ours for over twenty years when the husband passed away. His widow was suffering from stage four kidney failure, and only dialysis was keeping her alive. She came into our office with her son. Let us just say what a somber moment it was. This was during what could be her final stretch of life, and we all knew it.

We sat with them, and our client revealed to us that despite being a present parent and grandparent who loved her family endlessly, she felt like a disappointment. She thought she was leaving her family stranded because she didn't have a larger legacy gift for them. The whole office was in tears as this kind woman broke down and admitted how powerless she felt to do enough for her kin.

Her son felt differently, however. He was incredibly grateful to her for being such an outstanding parent. It wasn't about money, not to him. Despite his reassurances to his mother, she was actively trying to participate and be helpful in her own legacy gift. He kept repeating to his mom, "That's all you can do, and it's great, Mom. It's enough."

Interestingly, we had already established a plan for her fifteen years prior. By all measures, her legacy gift was quite generous! But she was in her last days, and in her illness, she had fallen into a "shoulda-coulda-woulda" kind of desperate thinking. Her son, with our moral support and confirmation of what her legacy was, managed to calm and comfort his mother.

By holding a family meeting to tell heirs and loved ones who your planner is, you can make passing on your legacy easier. This client and her late husband had no secrets from their son about who to consult when their time came. That is why her son caught that ball and ran with it—he brought his worried mother to confirm what they both already knew about her legacy. Watching the two of them hug, knowing that everything was in place as it was supposed to be, knowing that this lady could live her remaining days with that peace of mind was a priceless moment of proving to us that we were and are in the right business.

Clients have come to us with stories about trying *in vain* to get in touch with their portfolio manager, their retirement planner, or their financial advisor. Our clients have no difficulties or obstacles in booking meetings with us. We are here for our clients and their loved ones.

It's comforting to know that you have holistic retirement professionals on your side while you're alive and after you are gone.

As much as technology is replacing both professions and whole industries, a digital app can't be the name and face that's present for your kids when you pass away. An AI robot can't replace the emotional connection that a human planner brings to your retirement plan. That's why it's so important to find a retirement planner you can trust, who will be there for you and your next generation. We've been here for fifty years. Our business is not going anywhere anytime soon.

CHAPTER 6

PLANNING PROFESSIONALS VERSUS DIY

Now that you've read a little basic information about retirement planning (and you'll know more by the time you get to the last page), you might be tempted to save a couple of dollars and do the planning yourself. Anyone who's ever tried to save a few dollars doing their own plumbing or their own electrical work knows that some tasks are best left to a professional—unless you're okay with the potential of needing an even more expensive fix after you end up breaking or short-circuiting something.

Working with a Retirement Planner

We'll give you a story or two about new clients who came to us in desperate hope we could "fix" their do-it-yourself

(DIY) attempts to manage their own retirement funds. That's the first downside to a DIY approach to retirement wealth planning: You don't know what you don't know—until you fail.

Let us just remind you here that we never charge you for a consultation with one of us. Never. So why not just come in and discuss things with us? The key is to work with a professional you trust. A professional can actually save you quite a bit more time and effort than you could ever save on your own.

There is a second downside to DIY retirement planning. Some financial decisions only give you one shot to decide, with no take-backs or do-overs. A second set of eyes before you decide can help look over your work and see if there's anything you missed, which in my experience, there often is. A professional can also give you the knowledge and information you might never have found on your own. Knowledge is power, but first you must possess it!

Making a mistake in retirement—for example, not identifying a risk and suffering from it—can cost you tens or even hundreds of thousands of dollars. Read the next several chapters if you don't believe this. A professional planner should work collaboratively with you, which means you still get to make decisions, but with guidance. It's still your money.

What Makes a Good Planner?

How do you know when you've found a good planner? We have mentioned the wide range of designations and certifications in the financial industry. We admit that it is a challenge. Here is a short list of features you could look for:

1. A true professional retirement planner will have your best interests in mind.

We have talked about finding a fiduciary. That means you come first. It means they sit down and listen to you. They take an interest in your retirement goals. They measure your risk tolerance. Then they'll look at where your money is and talk about risk and how to reduce it. They serve *your* financial interests, not their own.

2. The retirement planner must be an independent advisor.

Only an independent financial service professional can offer you a broad range of options (not just one) that work best for your goals and your risk tolerance.

Note that if your planner is a captive agent, working for a big corporation, they're always going to be obliged to sell that company's products. They will always be under pressure to meet a sales quota to keep their boss happy. That's a conflict of interest. That is not independence. They simply can't put your needs first. You want an independent advisor with access to a broad range of products (not all will suit you, but this type of advisor can talk to you about more than one company's products).

3. If you ask a good retirement planner how they are paid, they tell you.

Our clients ask us this all the time. It is a valid question. They know we're running a business. Because we don't charge to meet with them, they're wondering, "How do these people earn their money?" We (and every other advisor should) tell them. We're transparent about it.

4. The retirement planner's approach must be holistic.

They can provide risk-reduction planning, estate/legacy planning, and income/spending planning, and they can educate you all along the way.

This is the holistic approach that we at Bostian Retirement Planning LLC and Wingler Wealth Management have worked with our strategic partners to implement. To give you an idea of what's possible, here's an overview of all the services you can obtain after you walk in our front door.

Services that Bostian Retirement Planning and Wealth Management provides to clients (though we won't be talking about them all in this book) include:

- Annuities
- Asset protection
- Charitable giving strategies
- Controlled distribution to heirs
- Income planning
- IRA legacy planning

- Long-term care protection/insurance
- Social Security maximization
- Tax planning (tax minimization strategies)
- Wealth accumulation strategies

Services that Chris (operating as Wingler Wealth Management) provides to clients include:

- Investment allocations designed to address your goals and risk tolerance
- Retirement planning
- IRA and 401(k) rollovers
- Stretch IRA planning (limited to eligible beneficiaries)
- Tax planning (tax minimization strategies)
- Wealth accumulation strategies and planning

Services that our strategic partners provide (while we work closely with them) include:

- Estate planning
- Inherited IRA trust
- Life insurance and irrevocable life insurance trusts (ILIT)
- Probate avoidance
- Revocable living trusts
- Special needs trusts

5. A good retirement planner is available to their clients.

Your financial professional should not be invisible after that first meeting. They welcome a long-term relationship with you. They want to hear about life changes and help you plan to adapt to them.

We've been in business since 1976. We don't just have relationships with our clients, but also with their children, and now their grandchildren. These relationships bring deeper meaning to the work we do, and our clients feel it, see it, and know it. That is why 100 percent of our new business comes through referrals.

If your current planner doesn't meet all five criteria, come see us. We do.

Just remember that all our consultations are complimentary. We'll answer your questions. We can give you more education during later meetings with you to correct any misinformation you might have. We can make suggestions and present strategies that get your retirement funds organized to your benefit. When we say, "to your benefit," we mean that we organize your money to meet your goals with a focus on minimizing unnecessary risks.

PART THREE

THE BASICS OF RISK

Risks, you ask? Oh, yes. There are more kinds of risk to your retirement money than most of our new clients can name. However, they can name all the risks once we've educated them! They also hear about our strategies that are designed to reduce those risks.

Raymond says, "Clients hesitate to consult only because of some misconceptions. They think this is very complicated, or it's going to be very expensive, or we're trying to sell them something. We're professional retirement planners. We help all our clients have a better retirement because we protect their retirement funds."

Read on so that you can learn what we know about risks, and then you can ask us about strategies that are designed to help protect your hard-earned money from unnecessary risks.

CHAPTER 7

TAXES ARE A RISKY BUSINESS

Back in Raymond's dad's day, when people retired with a pension and Social Security, there was no mystery. Those two sources of income were steady throughout retirement, and so was the amount of taxes due on them. If people had savings, it was often in the bank, and they'd already paid tax on that.

Today, though, one of the biggest financial problems a person has in retirement is taxes. It is such a problem that we call it a risk.

Tax risk? That's a shocker for most folks.

Most people come to us believing, "Taxes are what Uncle Sam tells me. How can it be a *risk* if I can't do anything about it? It might feel like a *burden*, sure. But a risk?"

Not only do our clients generally not realize this as a *future* risk, but most of them also don't realize that there are two types (or sources) of tax risk. It is possible to manage both types. People can eliminate a lot of taxes perfectly legally. The catch? They have to plan.

Reducing or eliminating tax risk does mean early planning, often years in advance. But since people don't know about this risk, they never plan. They never seek out a trained tax planning professional. They don't have a CPA (which we are not, by the way) helping them plan. They think they've done their best.

This is another area where we need to educate clients: Filing or calculating your taxes for the current year is not tax *planning*. It is tax *filing*.

A tax preparer (think of those "We Do Taxes!" signs you see in late winter) will look back twelve months and say, "This is what you will file. This is what you will owe." That's a tax preparer. These professionals are needed, but here's the catch: They only look *back*.

Tax is a topic a lot of people are actually concerned about. On the other hand, we have clients who never saw taxes as a risk factor—not in their earning years, and not in retirement.

We certainly don't usually know what the tax rates or our future tax picture will be. None of us do. But not too many people know that their tax burden might be a shocking amount in retirement if they don't take action sooner. They don't know they need a tax *planner* who (contrary to that tax preparer) looks *forward* for you.

As we said, there are two versions of tax risk. The first type or source of tax risk is right in your tax-deferred accounts—your 401(k) account, your IRA, or any other tax-deferred accounts where you have retirement savings.

First, the RMD Tax Risk

As we've discussed, most retirement funds are in what we call pre-tax accounts. These are traditional IRAs, simple IRAs, solo and employer 401(k)s, 403(b)s, 457(b)s, SEPs, defined benefit pension accounts, and TSPs.

You can save taxes during your working years by using pre-tax accounts because then you don't owe the tax on that year's saved money until later.

Now, in retirement, you'll be drawing money from accounts that have never had any taxes paid on them. You have an immediate tax liability.

Most people just think, "It's Uncle Sam. I gotta do what I gotta do—and that's pay!"

If tax risk is about paying or not paying income tax, what is this *RMD tax risk*? RMD stands for "required minimum distribution." It applies to you when you have money in pre-tax accounts and you have reached age seventy-three.

The law requires you to take an RMD starting at age seventy-three. Every year, the IRS will tell you *how much you must withdraw* from those pre-tax accounts, and then you must also, of course, pay the tax right away.

When we pull money from an investment that we've already paid the taxes on (such as a bank savings account), when we need a dollar, we take a dollar and we are done. However, if we take it from a pre-tax account like an IRA, we have to do some calculations.

If you need $10,000, you can't just withdraw $10,000 from that pre-tax (tax-deferred) account and be done. You're not going to get $10,000—you still need to pay taxes on it. If we assume 22 percent federal income tax withholding at the time of the withdrawal, you would be left with $7,800. Clients come to us to figure out taxes that will be due and how much to take out so they have the $10,000 they need. While we're not CPAs, we do have strategic partnerships that we recommend to our clients and we will work with them to develop a long-term tax plan based on their assets, income, and goals in retirement.

This required withdrawal and tax-due issue starting at age seventy-three is what's called the RMD tax risk, also known as the "tax bomb."

Today, we're seeing earlier retirees. That gives us retirement income planners an opportunity to bring up this topic of tax risk when clients are in their late fifties to early sixties, right around the time that they're considering Social Security. That's the time when we would like to have those tax mitigation conversations with them. It would be too late to mitigate taxes if you were to start only at, say, age seventy-two. You're already in the thick of it at that time.

So, that's the risk. What's the solution or strategy to reduce that risk? First, you need a strategy to start managing that tax risk *today.* Second, you might need to reorganize your finances.

Your tax management strategy may include a Roth IRA account.

Roth Conversions

We like to start early and help you consider what is called a *Roth conversion*—a transfer from your tax-deferred account into a Roth IRA, after paying the tax on it that year. Then all qualified withdrawals from the new Roth account are tax-free going forward.

What's a Roth IRA account? It is a type of account usually invested in the financial markets. In this case, the money you put in the account is money you have already paid income tax on. That makes it different from, say, a traditional 401(k).

Keep in mind that Roth conversions involve paying taxes up front on the converted amount. The decision to convert should take into consideration your current and expected future tax rates.

Here's the double advantage: Growth and withdrawal are both tax-free. You can convert a portion of your traditional IRA or traditional 401(k) pre-tax money over several years into a Roth IRA. This will help spread out the tax burden over multiple years.

The Roth strategy is an advanced strategy to think about in your fifties or earlier. Doing this has, again, two advantages:

1. You pay taxes at a known tax rate because you and your planner have done the math.

2. Your money is now in a Roth IRA where it has the potential to grow tax-free. In later years, you can even withdraw the growth with no further taxes due on it. You and your planner can decide how to manage your portfolio for the growth you want based on your risk tolerance.

These are big conversations. These are hot topics with a lot of people. The tax will be due. There's no way around it. But you can, with planning, control when, and to some extent, how much tax you pay.

Some people have fifteen or twenty years where they could easily mitigate the tax burden. They save the money, and they cross the finish line. At that point, it's what you do with it. They may need some of the money early in their retirement or only when they're in their later seventies. It's up to them and their income plan.

Note this, though: When you hit age seventy-three, the delays disappear. From that birthday on, until your tax-due accounts are empty, it is going to be Uncle Sam telling you the minimum amount to withdraw each year. Uncle Sam doesn't care if you need that much or not. He wants his tax payment! You have to withdraw it and pay those taxes. Because, as we all know, Uncle Sam is the biggest "collection agency" in the world—and he has ways of collecting.

However, please consult us about your Roth conversion strategy. There are strategic ways to do those "conversions," and you have just seen one of them. We'll get into more good and bad ways in a minute.

It's true that some younger retirees don't want to talk about this long-term tax planning. What we would say to them is that it gives them more control. The majority of the people we run into don't know about tax planning versus tax preparation. They never imagined how the Roth IRA could potentially help them in retirement.

Long story short about the Roth, you can legally move some or all of your tax-deferred retirement plan money into the Roth. From then on, all money in the Roth can start growing tax-free.

Although the taxes do have to be paid up front, the Roth IRA still offers tax advantages that every retiree should discuss with their retirement planner.

Deciding on your own (a DIY approach) whether to do this conversion may be confusing. Deciding how much to convert (all at once or a little at a time over some years) will be confusing. To most people, making this decision and feeling confident about it may seem impossible. Here is why: Can you write down what your tax bracket will be in ten years, and how much taxable income you'll have then? How about for twenty or thirty years from now? *You don't have that information.* And without it, it's all too easy to make a suboptimal decision. You would never try to give yourself a root canal. And while you could try to do your own Roth conversions, you'll quite likely be better served by a professional. Anyone who attempts to calculate their future tax picture on their own runs a big, expensive risk: losing a sizable chunk of their retirement portfolio to taxes.

Most DIY people don't reorganize their finances for tax efficiency because they don't know about this so-called "tax bomb." That is why we plan with you. It's essential to build your tax plan. A tax plan looks at which of your assets are taxed and which are not.

Here is an over-simplified RMD-reduction strategy in a nutshell: Draw from the taxed assets *until you've reached your desired tax bracket.* Then draw from assets that aren't taxed. Pretty simple, right?

Except for one detail. Do you know how to figure out those numbers? Probably not, as we just said.

Let's look at those numbers. Education first! Remember that your numbers will be different, but the strategy will be the same. The following is the IRS 2025 tax rate table for a single taxpayer.[5]

---

5   Andrew Lautz, "2025 Federal Income Tax Brackets and Other 2025 Tax Rules (2026 Filing Season)," *Bipartisan Policy Center*, January 29, 2026, https://bipartisanpolicy.org/explainer/2025-federal-income-tax-brackets-and-other-2025-tax-rules/.

Tax Rate	Taxable Income Bracket, Single	Tax Liability, Single
10%	$0-$11,925	10% of taxable income under $11,926
12%	$11,926-$48,475	$1,193 + 12% of income from $11,926-$48,475
22%	$48,476-$103,350	$5,579 + 22% of income from $48,476-$103,350
24%	$103,351-$197,300	$17,651 + 24% of income from $103,351-$197,300
32%	$197,301-$250,525	$40,199 + 32% of income from $197,301-$250,525
35%	$250,526-$626,350	$57,231 + 35% of income from $250,526-$626,350
37%	$626,351+	$188,770 + 37% of income above $626,350

Amounts rounded to the nearest dollar. Taxable income = adjusted gross income minus deductions. For example, a married couple with $61,500 in adjusted gross income who claim the $31,500 standard deduction would have $30,000 in taxable income.

Here's how that strategy would work for a single person with taxable income of $58,000 per year. Look at your income this year.

$48,475 - $58,000	This portion is taxed at 22%
$11,925 - $48,475	This portion is taxed at 12%
$0 - $11,925	This portion is taxed at 10%

From no income to $11,925, you pay a 10 percent tax. Add to that tax amount that your income from $11,925 to $48,475 is taxed at 12 percent. Add to that the tax on your earnings between $47,151 and $58,000, which is taxed at 22 percent. As you can see, there are some very steep hikes from one bracket to the next one if you're not careful about which assets you draw from. If you then decide you need additional income this year, and withdraw, say, $20,000 from a tax-deferred account, that $20,000 is going to be taxed at 22 percent. The chart says it: You're still in the 22 percent bracket. Any income from $47,151 to the new amount of $78,000 will be taxed at 22 percent. That $20,000 did not spike you into the next higher, 24 percent bracket.

Where Is Your Risk? Where Is Your Safety?

Now you need to know which of your assets are prone to spiking your tax bracket and which are not. We can help you create your future-looking tax plan in advance and calculate how you could best generate your retirement income.

To sum it up, here's how the following types of assets compare in terms of taxes.

1. Checking and Savings

This is cash. It is the money deposited in your checking and savings accounts. It's the money in a cash deposit account. It is your money. You have already paid taxes on it to even get it into those accounts. That means you don't have to claim it as income or pay more income tax on it. This allows you real flexibility when it comes to withdrawing money from these accounts as needed to supplement your taxable income and stay in a lower tax bracket.

This is a no-more-tax-due type of money (any interest earned on this money is still taxable).

2. Social Security

Although not considered an asset, this is your monthly check or direct deposit that you get from the government. This is tax-preferred income, which means Social Security income *may* be partially taxable. Up to 85 percent of your benefit *may* be subject to federal income tax. That will depend on your total income level.

This is a some-tax-may-be-due type of money.

3. Traditional IRA and 401(k) Plans

These accounts were great while you were saving for retirement. They do, however, come with a downside due to their tax-due status. That's a double problem: 1) Tax is due on all distributions. 2) You want to withdraw from them, but now you need to consider how much extra you need to withdraw for spending needs and for taxes!

On top of that, Uncle Sam forces you to take a required minimum amount from these accounts beginning at age seventy-three, which can push you into a higher tax bracket than you prefer.

This is a taxes-always-due type of money. This is true once you have voluntarily withdrawn it or only withdrawn it because Uncle Sam said so!

4. Roth IRA

Roth accounts are IRA plans that allow you to pay your taxes *before* you put the money in. This money (even the gains—*unlike* your personal trading account holding your valuable stocks) doesn't count as income. There is no required minimum withdrawal amount.

This is a no-tax-due type of money.

So Many Questions!

These are the questions we get most often about RMD tax reduction strategies:

- "Where's the best place to offset this withdrawal for taxes?"
- "When is the best time to do it?"
- "How much should we convert this year or next year for the least taxes?"

Sit with us, give us a 360-degree view of your financials, and let us crunch the numbers with you. Then you can decide based on that knowledge.

We repeat and repeat it: At Bostian Retirement Planning and Wealth Management, we are educators. In fact, we might as well rename our company: Bostian Retirement Educators!

You have to pay the tax any way you cut it. The Roth conversion strategy gives you control of when you pay taxes. If you're expecting to be in a higher tax bracket in retirement, then converting early is worth considering.

Second, the Liquidation Risk

The second type (source) of tax risk to you is for those of you with personal trading accounts and any type of investments. Maybe you opened an E*TRADE account years ago, and you put a little money in it to open the account, and maybe you added a couple of thousand per year after that. Maybe you invested it on your own with some dividend-paying stocks. Maybe you just went to a broker and said, "I have $10,000; invest it, please."

Now let's be clear. You had already paid tax on the money you put into those accounts. So where is the tax risk?

We don't have many clients in the following situation (but don't we all wish we had done this?), so let's call this a hypothetical and somewhat "wishful thinking" example.

Say you worked in technology in the very earliest years of that industry. Why not invest in Microsoft? So you do. With an initial investment of just $150 in Microsoft at the very earliest stock price of $21 per share in 1986, you could buy only seven shares. Not many, right? But still, you never touched the shares, and thirty-nine years have gone by. In that time, the stock has split nine times, bringing the number of shares you now own to 2,016 shares. Wow! 2,016 shares times the current share price of $509 (as of September 16, 2025) is equal to $1,026,144. Wow, wow, wow.

But guess what? Everything over the initial $150 invested is taxable as long-term capital gains when you liquidate (cash out) some of your shares. That is what we at Wingler Wealth Management call *liquidation tax risk*.

Likewise, if you or your broker invested your money in dividend-paying stocks, you pay the tax on those dividends the year they are credited to your account. If you earn only a few hundred dollars in dividends, your tax picture probably won't change much. But what if you earn tens of thousands of dollars in dividends? That could be a tax risk to plan for because it might pop you into the next higher tax bracket.

Chris is an investment advisor representative. In collaboration with our referral to an estate attorney, he will have some strategies for you to mitigate and potentially even eliminate this liquidation risk. Some of the strategies for reducing this liquidation tax risk are for charity-minded individuals, while others are for those with a strong interest in leaving a financial legacy to their heirs and beneficiaries. That's all we'll say for now, since it is a personal and sometimes advanced strategy, but just know that strategies to mitigate this risk exist.

The Strategy Is Estate Tax Planning

In the end, what we're talking about here is *estate tax* planning. Now you know from writing up your TEP with our attorney that a total estate plan is about forward thinking. Your TEP answered those "what if" questions about the future.

This is planning for your retirement years, but also for your heirs. *Tax planning* is about looking forward. Tax planning is looking into the next ten to thirty years to plan the best way to reduce, or eliminate, as much tax as we can. And again, this is legitimate. It is allowed.

As we mentioned, we don't do tax filing at Bostian Retirement Planning and Wealth Management, but with the help of our training and support from the Ed Slott organization,[6] we do tax planning. We're not tax *planners* because we're not CPAs or a tax firm. But with the help of Ed Slott, we do tax planning on your tax-due retirement accounts, and there's no fee for that to any of our clients.

Here is the bottom line: Taxes are one of our biggest retirement income planning challenges. Most people don't even have that on their radar as something to be aware of.

The best way to reduce your tax burden is to look forward many years into the future.

It may sound counterintuitive that you spent your life paying taxes, but then you still have to pay taxes during retirement as well. Or do you? We'll see. Keep reading.

We had a very nice client who had been a widow for almost two decades when she decided to retire from her part-time nonprofit job. She mostly kept it because she loved the impact she made on society.

---

6   Ed Slott and Company LLC, "America's IRA Experts," https://irahelp. com/. Slott has been recognized by *The Wall Street Journal* as "The Best Source for IRA Advice" (https://irahelp.com/timebomb) and has been quoted as a tax planning expert by *The New York Times* and many other reputable news sources (https://irahelp.com/aboutEdSlott.php). Both of us are in Ed Slott's Master Elite Advisor group, and he helps us do tax planning for our clients.

With her husband, and since his passing, she'd always tried to DIY her life whenever possible. Managing her finances was no different. Truthfully, she hadn't even looked at her husband's 401(k) plan when he passed because the money didn't mean anything to her. In other words, she didn't need it.

When she came to us at retirement time, she thought she had a few million dollars in investments. She was pretty sure, but not 100 percent confident, that the amount would be more than enough for her to live well through retirement.

The first thing we saw from her financial organization was her *tax liability*. She had filed her taxes diligently every year and qualified for a good Social Security payment. Oh, she was up to date with the tax man.

But after looking at the whole picture and running some numbers with her, she wasn't expecting this shocker! She would lose much of her money if she didn't make a very strategic, forward-looking tax plan. Her current financial setup ran both of the tax risks we just discussed.

As we guided her toward a better strategy, this sharp widow became incredibly grateful for the new knowledge. She thought she knew, but as we always say, *she didn't know what she didn't know—until she knew it.*

After educating her about how her financial retirement would play out with no tax plan versus with a tax plan, she was astonished. Let us just say that after only a few meetings and a couple of minor adjustments to her assets, she was going to walk away with almost *20 percent more of her money* than if she had tried to do it herself.

A few years later, this lady came back to us with a new husband in tow. We helped walk them both through their new retirement plan. We gave him the same two-tax-risks education we gave her, and he gently reorganized his finances with our guidance—and to his benefit. It was a real pleasure to see such a good person have the happiness and abundance she deserved and enjoy a healthy financial future.

So those are the two biggest tax risks that we discuss with all our clients. Hold on to your hat, though, because your lessons about risk are not finished. Keep reading for more education about risks to your money.

CHAPTER 8

MARKET-RELATED RISKS

In Chapter 7, we spoke about sources of tax risk in your retirement. You now know you should talk to us early about strategies that are designed to reduce those risks.

There are more kinds of risk we need to explain. But please, don't throw this book in the dumpster! This is education for you. Keep reading, and you'll know more about risks to your retirement funds than many Americans. Why? Because fewer than 5 percent of Americans ever read books about their retirement or financial planning.[7] Moreover, most retirement-aged Americans flunk a "Retirement

---

7   Bob Haegele, "Only 4% of Americans Read Books for Money Advice - Here's Where You Should Start," *Yahoo! Finance*, May 25, 2023, https://finance.yahoo.com/news/10-classic-money-books-everyone-210013679.html.

Income Literacy" test.[8] Right this moment, you're reading more books about retirement than 95 percent of Americans ever do!

If you have money in the financial markets, you have invested in securities—stocks, bonds, ETFs, mutual funds, etc. This means you have a portfolio. Chris believes securities portfolios require risk management. Risk mitigation (reduction) is the whole purpose of Wingler Wealth Management. This is also known as investment allocation management; as an investment advisor representative, Chis is able to assist with this. Here we are also talking about planning as far in advance as you can.

First, though, let's look at what *market risk* actually is. It goes beyond the tax risk we just discussed. Like tax risk, it is multi-faceted, requiring you to pay attention to all facets.

Market Risk

Let us give you our math example of how we check out your mindset and understanding. It also explains market risk to you.

This risk is different from that fun tech stock example you read in Chapter 7. This math applies to all money invested in the financial markets, including your tax-deferred retirement accounts.

---

8   Kerry Hannon, "Most Americans Flunk When It Comes to Retirement Literacy, Study Finds," *Yahoo! Finance*, February 24, 2024, https://finance.yahoo.com/news/most-americans-flunk-when-it-comes-to-retirement-literacy-study-finds-140518119.html.

Here's how our talk with clients goes: "We want to show you some fifth-grade math, and we want you to participate. This is not cheesy. It's real math. Our goal is to educate you about a problem that you could have that you don't even know about. You don't know because your stockbrokers may not have told you."

We go into that fifth-grade math with "What's one plus one?" They'll grin and say two. We say, "What does one minus one equal?" They'll say zero.

We say, "Perfect. Let's talk about stock market math now. If you've got $100,000 and the market goes down 50 percent and then it comes back up 50 percent, how much money do you have now?"

And they'll say, "Well, wait, we're back at $100,000."

No, they aren't. They're at $75,000. They're sitting at minus 25 percent of their money. Almost everyone looks puzzled at that. We spell it out.

- The market goes down 50 percent, and you have $50,000 left.
- The market goes up 50 percent, but you only have $50,000 left.
- Your $50,000 goes up 50 percent—and 50 percent of $50,000 is $25,000.
- Add the original $50,000 to the latest market increase of $25,000, and you now have $75,000.
- You're minus 25 percent from your original value.

Even though the market went down 50 percent and back up 50 percent, you've lost. Most people know the markets rise and fall. They don't know this math, though, until we do this with them.

The next thing you see is plain as day. When you're in retirement and you have $100,000 and you're taking out $10,000 for income, and then the market goes down 50 percent (while extremely rare, it has in times past), you may run out of money before the market comes back.

We ask them how much of their money they're willing to lose. Almost all say, "None!" We educate them. We might say, "By looking at your current existing portfolio with the broker, you're not positioned right."

We consider ourselves "safe" retirement income planners. We tell every client that our goal is to change their family's life forever for good. We can take what Warren Buffett has always said to the bank. He said investors have to obey just two major rules:

Rule #1: Don't lose money.

Rule #2: Never forget Rule #1.

What we described in Chapter 7 was the tax risk to your invested money—how much Uncle Sam will take for himself from your invested money and realized gains in the account.

What we've just described right here is market risk. Market risk is the potential for losses on your investments due to various factors that affect the financial markets.

You may have heard the phrase, "timing the market," and it just means that people who actively trade to make money are trying to *predict* which way the market will move. Will it go up or down? Frankly, most people are just awful at timing the market.

Related to that is a risk to you, and it's about *when you retire.*

Sequence-of-Returns Risk

When any client comes to us with all of their money in a 401(k) or in a regular trading account, that money is all in the market. You'd be surprised how many people don't realize that there's a dangerous risk to their market-invested nest egg *in the years before and during retirement.* We like to be careful in the five years before and the five years after your retirement date.

When we think about the market going down. The questions about that are:

- when,
- by how much, and
- how long will it stay down?

The stock market goes up and down, sometimes dramatically. Sometimes, when it goes down, it stays down for years. That's risky if all your money is in the stock market and you're a couple of years away from retiring! Our clients see the need for sound advice when they understand that their money is at this kind of risk.

There is always a risk that your portfolio value will go down. You could lose money that you thought would pay your bills in retirement. That is, as we have revealed, market risk.

There is a related risk called the *sequence-of-returns* risk. What is that? Say you retire just as the market crashes. You certainly didn't time the market because you had no idea how to do that! It was (and usually is) the luck of the draw.

If you're overly invested in the market, you will be taking distributions while the market is down—just as you retire! It could mean that you need to put off your retirement for five to ten years while the market recovers or take a big financial hit and live on less money for the rest of your days. That is the sequence-of-returns risk. You hoped for positive returns all through retirement. You got negative returns right at the start of your retirement years. Your accounts could have less money.

When the dust has settled, the order of investment returns may have impacted your retirement savings significantly. If you go through negative investment returns early in retirement (the market is declining), it can deplete your portfolio faster. This makes it harder to recover in subsequent years. This "didn't/couldn't time the market" risk is the sequence-of-returns risk, and if you need to take distributions from your investments, it's a risk to your money at the wrong time.

There was an investment news article that came out back in 2005 about these two brothers—we'll just call them Arthur and Zack—who had the same portfolio structure. In other words, they both had about the same amount of money, and it was all invested the same way. Arthur retired before Zack. Arthur did really well in retirement, money-wise. Zack retired some years later and saw a big chunk of his money just evaporate from his portfolio due to a sequence-of-returns disaster.

How could that be? When Arthur retired, we'd been in a rising stock market, a bull market, for a while.

But by the time Zack retired, that upward trend had ended. What was worse, the market started declining badly in the first months after he retired, eating his portfolio away. Because he didn't reallocate any of his funds, he ended up running out of money.

When you enter retirement, the distribution or spending phase of your financial life, you aren't putting any new money in the pot. Quite the contrary! Now you're pulling money out. Market declines are more of a detriment to you at this point. If you have too much money in too many correlated investment instruments, you could be in trouble.

This is the sequence-of-returns risk, and it is about timing. Now you know that no one can always get it right! This sequence-of-returns risk is why you need asset allocation management.

Well, that is market risk and sequence-of-returns risk. Let's talk about how we help our clients reduce that risk.

Asset Allocation Risk

In some of our stories, you've detected problems with our client's portfolio. What you detected was a set of investments that may not have taken into account the client's goals and risk tolerance. Those investments didn't help the client achieve all their goals and might have put their retirement funds at unnecessary risk of loss.

Chris's investment management work is called *Asset allocation management*, the purpose of which is to match your investments to your goals and work to mitigate investment risks.

Chris often sees that our new clients' portfolios, when they have more than one account, frequently overlap. He might see that their previous advisor designed with entirely too much safety or entirely too much risk. They might have two different portfolios that are really accomplishing the same thing.

Chris looks at the overall picture—all of their money—and makes sure they don't have any overlapping sectors or overlapping goals.

We had a new client come in who thought he wanted to allocate more toward safety in his market portfolio. Chris looked at the statements he brought in. Instantly, he saw two things:

1. He didn't realize how much safety his prior advisor had *already* built in for him through

annuities. This gentleman was looking at only one of his accounts, not his overall wealth.

2. He didn't realize the significance of where the money in his managed portfolios was invested. It was mainly *bonds.*

We did know the significance of that allocation. Contrary to the older couple we spoke about who had too much risk and no reward, this client had too little risk, producing too little reward!

Chris took this new opportunity to educate him. His advisors were accomplishing the same goal—safety—in two different portfolios. If you consider annuities and bonds, you might still be thinking, "Guys! He's invested in safe money. What's the problem?"

Well, there is *safe.* And then again, there is *too safe!* Let us explain.

We explained to this gentleman how "safe" or conservative these investments really were. We also told him that he was missing out on potential growth that the market could provide. How? He literally had none of his money in growth stocks or growth instruments. Chris explained that, invested like this, he would have a hard time beating future inflation; the longer he lived, the less money he'd have; he had no wiggle room for legislative or policy risks down the road (more on those types of risk next).

He then wanted to know how Chris would reorganize his money for a better balance between gains and protection to fit his individual circumstances. The rest of our discussion was around just that: managing inflation risk and market risk while still maintaining some safer assets.

All Under One Roof

You now know that Chris is a investment advisor representative, which makes him a fiduciary. While Raymond is not legally considered a fiduciary, he does hold himself to the same fiduciary standard. This puts all the retirement wealth-planning services you might need under one roof. Our clients get the convenience of working with a retirement income planner (Raymond) and a financial advisor (Chris) under the same physical roof for both insurance and investment needs.

The Securities and Exchange Commission (SEC) is very particular about how we work with clients and their portfolios. Chris has to notify clients when he sits down with them that he is licensed on both sides. Chris has two separate business cards for that reason. If we have a client who has questions about securities, Chris will take that as a separate meeting. He has a completely separate appointment about securities where he dives into investments and answers those questions.

The SEC requires that information about clients he has in the securities portion of the business remain completely separate from all of our insurance clients to make sure that there's no information transfer. Chris has a dedicated administrative staff who are the only ones that can actually touch these files. No information transfer is clearly something that the SEC is concerned about. We have separate file cabinets for these clients—that is actually a requirement for us.

As far as client confidentiality goes, we are firm. We get asked for referrals all the time, where the person wants to talk to a client about "what we did for them." Absolutely not. We wouldn't want what another client did to meet their goals to drive you to us or away from us. We customize every retirement plan. There is no cookie-cutter portfolio. We never share what any client's money is doing or how or why. We never talk about any client's business to anyone except our own staff assigned to that client's account. Not ever. The SEC is very particular about all of that, and so are we. We think it is a good thing.

We let our clients know that not all people practicing in this industry are classified as fiduciaries. Chris is, and Raymond holds himself to that standard. If those others are not an active fiduciary, they aren't legally obliged to put the client's needs above their own.

At Bostian Retirement Planning and Wealth Management, we do things differently. You're educated on this important topic of risks to your money. Not all advisors bother with that education. We believe risk is a good aspect of their money management for our clients to understand, so we teach people about it. Because after all, who else do they know that can explain these aspects of their money to them?

Though we hate to say it, this topic of risk is not yet complete. No! Don't throw the book in the trash can down the street! Keep reading. We don't think you'll regret a minute.

CHAPTER 9

SNEAKY RISKS TO MANAGE

We take our job seriously. That job is to identify risks, explain them to you, and present ways to reduce or (when possible) fully eliminate a risk. We don't choose a solution for you. We give you information and options so you can make the final decision.

Whenever we sit down with our clients and ask what their tax picture will be in five, ten, or twenty years, they just go quiet. They don't know what a risk it might be until we tell them where the risk is—and our solutions to reduce it.

Likewise, we do the fifth-grade math you saw with all our clients. We may have scared you with that sequence-of-returns risk. Then we reassured you that Chris was an investment advisor representative. He has strategies to address market and timing risks.

Once in retirement, you don't get a do-over if your portfolio gets destroyed because you didn't know it was in danger. The sad truth is that many good people who were getting ready to retire had to rethink everything when the market crashed in 2000 and again in 2008. There were also repercussions due to the COVID-19 pandemic, with not only the market crashing then bouncing around but also with the ensuing inflation, which is still an irritant to many Americans' budgets as we write this in 2026.

Will the market crash in your retirement? We've experienced eleven recessions since 1948, or about one every six or so years.[9] If you spend the next twenty years in retirement, yes, you can expect the market to go down at times. You may also experience a recession again.

We have discussed tax risk. We have discussed market risk. Brace yourself. We are going to identify more risks to become aware of and manage. And rest easy! They are also manageable—with planning.

Let's list and describe the remaining common risks, and in the next chapters, we'll present some strategies to them.

Longevity Risk

This risk relates to the uncertainty of how long you're going to live. Will you be a centenarian? Will you live the longest

---

9   Kimberly Amadeo, "History of Recessions in the United States: Causes, Length, GDP, and Unemployment Rates for Every U.S. Recession," *The Balance*, updated July 9, 2024, https://www.thebalancemoney.com/the-history-of-recessions-in-the-united-states-3306011.

of anyone in your family history? You just don't know, and we don't have a crystal ball with the answer, either.

However, if you underestimate your life expectancy, you might exhaust your lump-sum retirement savings too soon. Isn't that most people's fear—running out of money before running out of life? No doubt, without planning, this could mean financial difficulties in your later years. And trust us, you don't want to be in your eighties or nineties and thinking about going back to work.

We've also told you some stories in prior chapters where we see that people are taking on too much risk for their age. Leaving all your money in the market is one such risk. Our new clients are often in this situation when they have come to us from a stockbroker. Remember the risk: If such a person is not a fiduciary, the risk is that this person may be acting in their own interest, not yours.

Withdrawal Rate Risk

Somewhat related to the previous risk, this risk refers to the rate at which you withdraw money from your lump-sum savings. If you withdraw too much too early in retirement— if you miscalculate your sustainable withdrawal rate—you could deplete your savings prematurely. When the money's gone, it's gone. This is a big one to watch out for, and we can help with that calculation.

One of the ladies on our staff was just patiently waiting in a checkout line in a grocery store when the man in front of her spontaneously turned around and started chatting.

Out of the blue, his first words were, "I retired last year with $450,000 in my 401(k). Now I've got $275,000 left. I don't know how I'm gonna make it my whole life." Then he turned away from her, leaving her stunned. A total stranger!

We don't know if this man arbitrarily spent the money on his own. We don't know if his family came around with their hands out and he just gave them money. We just don't know.

Here is what we do know: He was suffering from the withdrawal rate risk. (And why, oh why, was all his money still in a 401(k) after retiring?)

Legislative and Policy Risk

In your lifetime, there will likely be changes in federal and state tax laws. It's the way of our world. There might also be changes to Social Security benefits (either their amounts or the amount of taxes on them), health care policies, or pension regulations that can impact your finances and should be considered as potential risks.

Legacy Risk

The money you thought you'd leave to heirs might be at risk due to a lack of planning. We have shown you how to address this risk with our TEP in Chapter 1. You know now that if you pass away without having your estate documents in order, all of your assets could end up in a long and expensive legal process. At worst, the state could "inherit" everything if you don't have any living heirs. Don't skip Chapter 1!

Inflation Risk

As we write this in 2026, there is probably not one American right now who doesn't know how inflation feels.

Inflation is the general increase in prices over time, when our spending money has stayed the same. We say that "our money doesn't go as far as it used to." The three unknowns about inflation are:

1. when it will hit,
2. how long it will linger, and
3. how high it will go.

This is something you need to plan for by *reducing your risk*. If you have too much of your money in a fixed strategy, you may be getting beaten down by inflation. Your money may not be earning enough to match or exceed inflation. If your investment is earning 4 percent, and inflation is 7 percent, you lose.

If the rate of inflation outpaces your return on retirement investments, you might find it challenging to maintain your desired standard of living. In other words, if your money is worth less than it used to be, you're going to have less money to spend.

Because of the inflationary times we've gone through, more people are aware of the impact of inflation risk. Because we have Chris as a financial advisor, he can talk about risk and reward, and how he can reorganize investments to meet specific financial goals. Speak to Chris about reorganizing some of your investments.

Do-It-Yourself Risk

This is not an acknowledged risk in our industry, yet it is one we see more than we'd like.

A married lady came in to see us after a particularly worrisome time in her household's financial life. Her husband was a die-hard do-it-yourselfer, even in the complex activity called investing. He had wanted to earn as much as possible for their retirement, so he'd picked out some very high-risk and possibly high-reward stocks for his IRA. Less than a year from retirement, the two of them looked at a bleak market and discovered that the $250,000 he had set aside over the course of his career was now only $100,000.

Her husband didn't come to see us at first. He may have been too proud and frustrated at the loss. As they were already in their sixties, it was simply too late to leave all that money in the market and face more potential losses. They didn't believe—not anymore—that they could earn it back over the next decade.

We were able to help them reorganize their finances. We switched over their high-risk assets to safer retirement vehicles that wouldn't lose principal and came up with a monthly income/spending budget that they were happy with. They were still able to enjoy pretty much everything they were looking forward to in retirement. They just needed to set aside a little vacation fund that they contributed to every month, and their plan was complete.

Oh, yes, the gentleman finally did come in to talk to us with his wife. Now he's happy with their plan. He understands better now that it's always a good idea to get a second opinion! He and his wife had enough other assets allowing them to retire on time and still have plenty to look forward to. They didn't even have to pinch pennies, as she feared when she came to us.

He did learn the hard way about market risk and the risks of DIY! He accepted our educational talks about how to protect their money. Now they've limited and eliminated risk as much as possible across the rest of their retirement portfolio.

Nonprofessional Advice Risk

This is also not an acknowledged risk in our industry, yet it is most definitely one we hear about from new clients all the time. You can detect it in some of the stories we tell you about our clients.

It's you, listening to a nonfiduciary, nonprofessional retirement planner or advisor and following their advice. When you are listening to someone who is not a fiduciary, the risk is that you will be taking investment action in *their* interests rather than yours!

There's an old story in the financial industry. It is sort of an urban legend. It's called the 4 Percent Rule. It's supposed to be a strategy for making your money last your whole life. Well, we had this "nonprofessional advisor" story we used to tell about a retiree named Matthew.

He retired, and he simply left his money in his trading accounts with his stockbroker (who, we remind you, was not a planner and not a fiduciary). Having done that, he really didn't pay much attention to money matters. He told the broker to send him 4 percent of his money every year. After all, the broker had told him he'd be just fine with that amount.

Matthew was spending time with his grandkids and time on the lake. And as long as he got that 4 percent every year, he was okay. He didn't think a lot about it. He was "living the life," as he said.

Then one day, Matthew went to have breakfast at his local café, and the café's TV was on a financial news channel. The buzz was that the stock market was going down. Seriously down. Like more than 20 percent down!

Now we have hindsight. That was back in 2008, the Great Recession, though it wasn't called that right away. Matthew still didn't think twice, however. He just thought, "Well, I'm okay because my broker said we can always accomplish this 4 percent goal. It's no big deal." However, his broker called him. "Well, Matthew, we've had a little bit of an issue. The market's really gone down, so we're not going to be able to do your 4 percent. We're going to have to cut that off for a little bit until the market gets back and we can get you back to your 4 percent goal."

He had a choice, actually: not take any money at all or take 4 percent, knowing he would have much less cash for it than ever before. He took 4 percent, but it wasn't enough income. He had to go back to work. Matthew ended up having to sell the lake house.

Yes, this is the combined market risk and what we call nonprofessional advice risk. It can be painful.

When you have a "financial advisor" or "planner" who *tells* you how they are going to invest your money, run! When, as Matthew's advisor did, your advisor tells you how much and how to withdraw instead of asking you what your spending and other goals are, instead of managing all these risks you know about, run! If they are not a fiduciary, we often tell clients to take their money and run! Oh, yes, we've had to do that! Those are signs that you don't have the right retirement planner or the right financial advisor.

If you have a so-called retirement planner or financial advisor who tells you that they 1) manage your money and 2) also meet with you regularly, in my opinion, something is wrong, so run. I don't believe one individual can do both, though many out there do try. Some aspect of your business is getting dropped. I don't think there's any way somebody could manage client portfolios daily and also meet with clients day in and day out. Impossible. There's just not enough time in the day. That is why Chris utilizes the services of third-party money managers who are portfolio management professionals. This frees up Chris's time to meet with clients.

PART FOUR

THE BASICS OF A FINANCIALLY SECURE RETIREMENT

Part Three educated you on the risks that your money might face. Yet, when we talk with new clients, we find that

1. lots of people resist being told they are doing things wrong with their money; and
2. lots of people resist learning that their money may be at higher risk than they thought.

That's just fine because we are educators. You decide what to do with your money, but let us educate you about the risks, the various solutions, and your choices first. Some measure of risk might be suitable to reach your goals. More safe money might be what you need to sleep well at night.

Chris says, "For some people, consulting with us is checking off a box. One of the things that I enjoy most is being an educator to clients. We fill every void in their knowledge and planning. I think that's the most enjoyable part of this work—being part of their journey to a successful retirement."

Let us now educate you more on how we work to help you meet your retirement goals while also considering the risks you face.

CHAPTER 10

ALLOCATION MANAGEMENT

Under Wingler Wealth Management, Chris's wealth management and advisory goals are to create strategies that address your retirement goals and reduce unnecessary risks in your portfolio. How do we know how much risk you can tolerate with your money? We could guess that you don't want to lose a nickel of your nest egg. But guesswork is not our way of working with you.

This is another example of how we start with the end in sight. We don't have Chris make investment recommendations *first*. He does that *last*.

Evaluating Your Comfort with Risk

We start with a *risk analysis*. We do this assessment before we even know where you have your money. We want you to have a *risk reduction* and even a *risk elimination* mindset, and for that, we always start with *risk tolerance*.

How much tolerance do you have for loss? We find that our clients don't know this about themselves. Most don't know until we do this analysis.

We meet with plenty of people who insist, "Well, I'm very aggressive," but by the time we get done with the risk analysis, they realize that they're not as aggressive as they thought.

The risk analysis step is eye-opening when they compare their risk tolerance level to the actual risk their money is exposed to. You need to ask yourself, "Can I handle this amount of risk? What if I lose big, like in that fifth-grade math example and that sequence-of-returns example?"

You now know that you have risk everywhere you have money. You also know that you can reduce your risk with proper planning.

The Rule of 100

Back in the day, advisors followed a simple guideline known as the Rule of 100 when determining how to invest their clients' money based on risk tolerance. You subtract your age from 100. Say you are seventy-five; you subtract that from 100. The answer, 25, is the percentage of your assets that could go into *growth investments*, while your age, seventy-five, is the percentage of money that they would have in *safe-money investments*.

That 25/75 ratio seems pretty straightforward, and the advisor would change up the investments to meet the new allocation as the client aged.

For the past five to ten years, though, we've observed that the Rule of 100 doesn't work that well. Most of our clients have proven to be more conservative than the rule showed. Today, at Bostian Retirement Planning and Wealth Management, we use a couple of other tools with the Rule of 100 to get a more accurate reading of a client's comfort with risk.

A couple came in for a first appointment. At the time, they were both eighty-eight years old. They were really sharp and curious about a burning issue. They were referred to us by several of our clients. We were the third stop on their journey to find new advisors. Here was their burning issue: *Neither one of them knew where they had their money invested.*

Now, the Rule of 100 says 88 percent of their money should be in something that is safe, and 12 percent would be invested for growth (and some risk). However, when we did their risk analysis with our other tool, they came in at around a 40/60 ratio, not that 88/12. This 40/60 ratio is the range of a balanced investor.

You're going to be shocked to hear how they were allocated. They had 95 percent of their money at risk in the market. Not 95 percent safe—*95 percent at risk!* This had been true since 2014 with no changes at all.

They both looked to us for advice on what to do. We worked with this couple for a couple of months. It took a while because it was a very large case. Chris realigned their investments around their true risk tolerance. They were comfortable having some money (not most!) in the market, but he put them into a more balanced strategy for them that worked.

As with all our clients, we educated them. We explained. We gave examples. We ran the math for them. Their prior advisors had done none of that.

This couple followed along very well with all of it and soaked up the knowledge. They were amazed at our understandable explanations about risk, and they finally came to feel like they knew where their money was, how it was performing, and how those investments suited their goals (not to mention their actual tolerance for risk). They'd never had that before.

Safe Is Not What You Think

The majority of that couple's money was in different classes of bonds. Now, typically, people would think that bonds are safe. But as we've said, that's not always the case. Bonds are *conservative*, but not necessarily what we consider *safe*.

How so, if they were in bonds? The advisor had actually put them in the wrong type of bonds. We will spare you the details, but we'll just say that the term of their bonds was wrong, while the principal amount they invested in those bonds was fairly safe.

On top of those choices made on their behalf, those choices didn't even have any kind of conservative return on them. Although bonds can serve different purposes within a portfolio, this couple had made hardly any new money from those investments—for *years*. The bonds had virtually no growth at all up until two or three years before they met us, which was in mid-2023. This couple experienced multiple years of what I call "a failure to profit." As you saw, it is a real risk. There are thousands of stocks, bonds, ETFs, mutual funds, and other investment instruments. Managing risk involves utilizing various investment options that will help you obtain your investment goals while also staying within your risk tolerance.

Now, this business of money management is a lot to take in. We understand, and that's why Chris will walk you through every step.

Some people have heard from their advisor that they are in a "blended investment strategy," but they don't know what that means. It means they are holding money in various market segments (and we explain that to every client). It may not mean, however, that their money is safe!

Chris is securities licensed.[10] Most of our clients don't initially know what that means, and not every retirement planner is securities licensed. Having access to this service is one way we are different from the rest of them.

Those individuals with a securities license (such as Series 65) can legally provide investment advice, which can include advice about mutual funds, fee-based variable

---

10   As a general definition, securities-licensed professionals manage a wide variety of assets—not just stocks and bonds, but also mutual funds, ETFs, options, certain insurance products, commodities, and more, depending on their specific licenses. One example is the Series 65, which is required to provide investment advice or managing client investment assets for a fee.

annuities, stocks, bonds, and other such products. It also means that Chris can (and does) help with investment allocation management (also sometimes called portfolio restructuring), to align your investments to your goals and risk tolerance. This is a type of asset management that not all retirement planners can offer you.

Chris's securities license allows him to have a full discussion about your investment strategy. He can suggest new risk-reducing allocations for you as needed. As a *securities-licensed financial planning* professional, Chris is here to make sure that clients know what "risk versus reward" means for their investments.

We saw in Chapter 7 how there are strategies for liquidating gains in a portfolio and for potentially reducing RMDs as part of tax planning, and Chris advises clients on how to achieve this. Likewise, Chris makes sure that client portfolios—their investment choices—are aligned with their risk tolerance levels and their retirement and investment goals. Chris *plans* for the fact that there will always be ups and downs in the market. He also makes sure clients have flexibility based on what their needs are.

Having only securities—a stock market portfolio—is not a perfect strategy. Nothing is. We would attest to that. A perfect money strategy doesn't exist. There is no such thing as zero risk to your money. But combining different products and securities—stocks, bonds, ETFs, mutual funds, insurance, and so on—give you a measure of control where some of your money is potentially going to grow with current market times, while the rest of your money may be placed into vehicles with less risk such as insurance products.

Chris likes to do a portfolio analysis with every client. He sees what instruments you are investing in. He sees how your total invested money is allocated or divided between investment instruments and insurance products. He looks at the risks and the returns. He compares all that with your goals and with your level of risk tolerance.

Chris does this with new clients and reviews it every six or twelve months with current clients. Why? Because of a little-known but very real risk called "asset allocation risk." Allocation means placing varying amounts of your nest egg among different asset classes (types), such as stocks, bonds, or cash. The goal is to balance what everyone's heard of—risk and reward.

The main risk here is not that your money's in the markets. It's that it may not be in the allocation that will help you achieve your goals.

All this planning we do with you is about making sure you have your required amount of *net spendable* income to meet your retirement spending needs. You will be, at least in part, funding your retirement with money now in the markets. But you say, "Whoa! Wait! Aren't we supposed to reduce market risk and not have much money in the markets?"

You can keep money in the markets. But it should not *all* be in the markets. Remember those risks to your money we've already discussed.

This is the next level of planning we do. After all, you want to keep your hard-earned retirement assets. You don't want to give it up to Uncle Sam or lose it to unnecessary risk.

Knowing that you will be drawing retirement income from multiple resources, we'll recommend that you put your invested money into different types of assets. We call these *buckets* because they're easy to remember and make a lot of sense. (Think of the "all your eggs in one basket" saying. Instead of baskets, you have buckets.) You take some money from some buckets and leave money in others. Here are some examples of buckets. We'll keep it simple here and use three basic buckets.

Guaranteed Asset Bucket

Depending on your age, we will determine how much of your assets should be in the guaranteed asset bucket, in low-risk investments. That's because you want to have a certain portion that won't lose principal.

It's nice to have an emergency fund and some cash on hand at the bank as part of this bucket if you need it. The goal here is to also find some guaranteed or safe assets that have some opportunity for growth. Some of these types of assets can help you hedge against inflation or even draw down from the interest you earn rather than the principal.

Short-Term, Lower-Risk Assets

This is your some-risk bucket. These are assets in investments that aren't high on risk but offer better rewards than the really safe or guaranteed assets. Examples are a bond portfolio or a stable-value portfolio.

As long as you don't need to touch this money for five to ten years, it can be a part of your plan. As it performs well, you can rebalance and put some of your gains back into your no-risk bucket, while reinvesting another portion that you won't need to touch for a while.

Long-Term, Higher-Risk Assets

You can also put some of your assets from any of the three buckets "under management," which means an investment advisor representative like Chris is looking after them and ensuring that they continue to meet your goals and remain in line with your risk tolerance.

When you work with Chris to manage and organize all your money properly, you can put a portion of your money into safer assets and a portion into riskier assets that may give you some potential for more gains. That's the unique part of securities. The number one thing Chris discusses is your market risk in relation to your comfort with such risk. The securities portion of his work allows him to recommend investments that are aligned with your risk tolerance. Chris finds that often means restructuring your finances and investments. That brings us to our education of the client again. He demonstrates how the investments work, the levels of risk, and so on. He'll educate. You decide.

CHAPTER 11

A SAFER RETIREMENT PLAN

The first way to reduce risk is to know it exists. The hardest thing about risk is that without education, we're usually not aware of how exposed we are until we experience loss. That is why we encourage you to read and re-read those chapters in Part Three. Retirement is not a fun time to learn the hard way and make money mistakes—you have just seen all the distressing ways your financial retirement can go sideways. You know that under one roof, we not only educate you about the risks to your money but also provide strategies designed to reduce or eliminate those risks.

Sir Edmund Hillary is historically known in mountain-climbing circles. He and his sherpa (guide) Tenzing Norgay were not just the first people to climb Mount Everest all the way up to that summit. They were also the first people to successfully *make it all the way back down, healthy and safe.*

It's actually the descent that is treacherous, much more so than going up.[11] Ask any avid mountain climber.

Consider that as an analogy for retirement. Like most people, you get there just fine. You've hiked up that hill to the place called "last day of work, first day of retirement." For decades, you've saved. You reach age sixty-five and step across that finish line. You leave the job. But now what? You're on the long, long downward slope of life called retirement. Do you walk down safely?

We are safe-money advisors. As we always caution clients, there is no such thing as "risk-free." However, with our help, you can foresee and reduce many risks to your nest egg. You can work through each risk with us and decide which of the strategies we present will work for you. We may need to reorganize your assets—all of your finances— to avoid risk. Such risk reduction involves looking ahead, sometimes years, so that you can reorganize your finances and potentially add some protections. That is what financial planning is all about. That is what risk management is all about. That is what we do for you as safe-money retirement income planners.

---

11   "How Many People Have Died on Mount Everest? What Every Traveller Needs to Know (2025 Update)," *Nepal Outdoor Expeditions*, September 25, 2025, https://nepaloutdoorexpeditions.com/blog/how-many-people-have-died-on-mount-everest-what-every-traveller-needs-to-know-2025-update.

Get Down the Mountain Safely

We're still not done planning. Retirement is a broad concept, with dozens of moving parts. You are probably beginning to realize this! We believe there's too much for one person alone to keep track of. On top of that, you just don't know what you don't know—until you know it. That means that if you're trying to plan your financial retirement on your own or with the wrong type of advisor, you might discover some important piece of information too late. Once you have retired, there simply may not be enough time anymore to fully recover after a big financial hit.

When we explain how to help keep your money safe from those many risks we present, our goal is that you keep more of what you earned and saved. Our goal is always that you have more to spend and that your money lasts longer.

Safe Money

Rather than letting some other advisor or broker sell you on a bunch of products that may or may not work, our approach with you is to lean toward strategies that help you achieve your goals without taking on unnecessary risks. That means finding products that are lower risk, have lower or no fees, and may have tax advantages—all while meeting your goals and expectations. Safe-money strategies are financial approaches designed to protect your principal from market volatility or loss. You may see your money earn a lower percentage of interest or gains. It is still earning—safely earning. The more problems we can help you eliminate, the more hassle-free your retirement can be.

We are independent. That means we're not obligated to any one specific company's products, so we have access to a wide variety of products designed to address many different concerns.

Again, Chris is a fiduciary and Raymond holds himself to that same standard. That means Chris is legally obligated to only act in his client's best interest. We educate you so that you can decide. We never impose a strategy or financial move on you. We present our recommended retirement strategies, but you ultimately make the final decision. We just make sure you understand where your money is and why.

We would never recommend anything to you that we wouldn't recommend to our own mothers. Our goal is to help you protect your money before, during, and after retirement.

All this is why we're known as the safe-money guys.

Back to Asset Allocation

If you know the expression "don't put all your eggs in one basket," asset allocation is how to avoid doing that! Chris may recommend a portion of your retirement funds to potentially be invested. It has to be invested in a way that's comfortable for you.

In a stock portfolio, allocation is how you divide up your investments among different asset categories or types of stocks. Allocation means deciding what portion of the total portfolio is invested in various asset classes such as stocks, bonds, or cash. Allocation is also about managing risk and growth potential.

With most securities, you can buy into a security and sell right back out when it doesn't perform in the way you hoped. If a whole industry is suffering, and you own two companies in that industry, you can sell right away. Easy in, easy out. You move into something else. It just takes a phone call or a click of your mouse.

Securities are liquid—unlike, for instance, a piece of real estate. There is flexibility in securities. Since securities are liquid, they offer you more control over your income and spending management.

If you need to pay to repair damage to a car or have a sudden trip to pay for, you can liquidate some of the assets in these accounts to withdraw at the moment.

Some of our clients tell us they want to withdraw in order to buy what they call "their last car." We always laugh about that because we have heard the same clients say that perhaps two or three times and add, "And this time, I really mean it!" They're at an age where they realize that this "last car" costs more than their first house did some forty years ago. Think about it: $50,000 for a car today versus $20,000 to $40,000 for their first house!

If that is their goal, ours is to help them make it happen.

Why Safe Money Is Important

In a nutshell, you want safe-money products for:

- principal protection,
- steady or predictable income, and
- tax advantages.

Let's look at one of the safe-money solutions now. This is one that can be used for guaranteed income and still has potential to combat inflation. Turn the page and find out what it is.

CHAPTER 12

THE FIA—CREATE A RETIREMENT PLAN, NOT JUST AN INVESTMENT PLAN

We have come pretty far, and though we hate to say it (yes, you thought we had finished with this topic, so bear with us), there is one more risk to resolve. Well, a risk, yes, but more of a fear.

In fact, it is the most ingrained of our fears. In spite of all our education and planning up to this point, it lingers. What we do is address it head-on.

People are afraid of running out of money before they run out of life.

They look at that lump sum of money they've saved. Even though they've looked at their money in the market with Chris—even with the "three buckets" organization of that money—the fearful question is there.

"How can I take out this money to spend—but not spend it all before I die?"

It is a genuine concern we hear from new clients every week. It is really only that fear that keeps people up all night, nail-biting and worrying. They are fretting, "Will my money last as long as I do?" They are also worrying about whether the money they have coming in every month will pay the bills—not only today but also ten or twenty years in the future.

The Problem with Traditional Advice

Traditional advice can feel like a "one size fits all" approach. There's the Rule of 100, the 4 Percent Rule, and the 60/40 static asset allocation. These all assume that everyone's situation is the same and often ignore modern realities like longer life expectancies and current inflation or interest rates. We believe in building a customized strategy—one driven by your specific goals and your personal comfort with risk, rather than an outdated set of rules.

As your retirement income planners, it's our job to design a strategy that includes having enough income for all the years of your retirement. You want to be able to spend your money in retirement without fear of running out of income.

From Nest Egg to Income

In our discussions about income during retirement, we start with the amount of your total nest egg. Here's the difference that many people miss:

Income is not the same as a pot of money.

In our years of doing this work, we know the reason that people are afraid to retire. They no longer have a once-monthly or twice-monthly paycheck land in their bank account from their employer. The paycheck tells them exactly how much they have to spend that month. Easy enough.

With retirement, that's gone. Sure, there is our Social Security benefit that lands every month in the bank account. But we all know that was only intended as a supplement to other income in retirement.

Our process is straightforward.

1. We calculate your total spending for all bills and living expenses, plus the cost of your retirement activities. This is how much you need each month.

2. We look at your Social Security and your pension (if you have one). Those are guaranteed streams of income.

3. Then we do the math: *guaranteed* income minus expenses. Some clients have an income gap. They

have more expenses than guaranteed income. They know they could draw from those lump-sum accounts. That's where their sleepless nights start. What if that lump sum disappears and they still have an income gap?

Almost nobody we meet has ever used a written budget during their working years to manage their expenditures. Well, now is the time to write out how much you really spend every month. You can't create an income plan if you don't know how much you need to be spending.

The Strategy

We have one valuable strategy for you to consider to resolve this whole issue. The strategy we want to present now is of interest to anyone of any age with money they want to keep safe for retirement.

Annuities

In all the decades that Bostian Retirement Planning and Wealth Management has existed, *annuities* have been our main retirement *income* philosophy, tool, and strategy for making sure you have an income stream that's guaranteed for life.

Now, don't you go throwing this book into the Atlantic Ocean because of that word "annuities"!

Some people get all stirred up and say, "I wouldn't be caught dead with an annuity, no sir, no way!" That comes from misinformation. Stay with us, because it won't be what you think.

Remember, your pension works like an annuity. Your Social Security works like an annuity. Those are incomes that are yours for life, guaranteed. *They are your safe-money income streams.* Those are your retirement mailbox paychecks, but even with them, you may have an income gap.

So let's set the record straight about some types of annuities for you that can create income you can also count on for life. We have to tell you about them. We simply couldn't let you miss out on this retirement income planning strategy.

Investment Plan Versus Income Plan

Your number one goal during retirement is to not run out of money. That is where annuities play a part. Annuities can guarantee a mailbox paycheck for life—a guaranteed income that you can't outlive. There are annuities out there that work similarly to Social Security and pension money. You need to explore those now so that you address that income gap—and your fear of running out of money!

Social Security and pension money are what we call "mailbox paychecks." Every month, like clockwork, that income drops into your account. Guaranteed. No matter what the stock market is up to (or down to). No matter what taxes, interest rates, or inflation are doing. No matter how long you live.

It was Raymond who coined the phrase "mailbox paycheck." He founded the firm back when people did get their paychecks in the mail. Today, of course, our salaries and Social Security payments are direct-deposited into a bank account. But we would still love for all our clients to have a mailbox paycheck mentality about income in retirement.

A lot of our clients have tax-deferred retirement accounts with hefty sums in them. However, as we've discussed, to grow those accounts, people had them in the stock market. When they were young, that was fine. They had time for the market to go up and down, up and down—knowing that there was historically a long-term trend upward. We've discussed that and related risks and strategies to reduce them.

Here's the remaining issue: The 401(k) is an *investment* account. It's a lump sum of money sitting in the stock market.

That lump sum is not a mailbox paycheck. How can you turn it into a monthly income? How can your lump-sum nest egg provide you with a guaranteed mailbox paycheck?

That's the concern of every retiree: making sure that nest egg lasts.

When we first sit down with a client (actually in their third appointment, after they have their total estate plan (TEP) drawn up, funded, and properly in place), we ask them if they have an investment plan or a retirement plan with a "guaranteed mailbox paycheck." We ask to see their financial statements, which every client knows to bring in to us. They show us the statements.

Ten times out of ten, we'll be saying, "See here? You have an investment plan. It's all in the stock market. That's a straightforward investment plan. Do you understand it?" They usually do not. We ask, "What's the amount you've lost in the last year or two? Or since 2007 in general?" Of course, they had experienced declines at certain points because they were all in the stock market and experienced those bear markets; they might well have seen significant declines of their investments during those periods.

We tell them, "Let us explain a retirement *income* plan to you."

Yes, we talk first about how to address "risk" correctly—how having some money in the stock market would earn you some profits to potentially beat inflation. But the keyword is "some." The stock market is not where all your money should be in retirement.

Now, we also sometimes ask a client, "When you get in retirement, would you rather be rich or would you rather have an absolute guarantee that you'll always have an income stream?" The question makes some people laugh—until they remember their fear of running out of money in retirement. Then they are all ears.

We see people who are over sixty who still have their million dollars or their $640,000 or their $225,000 in an investment account. We believe having all of your retirement funds in one account is not the best approach.

Why not? Remember in the Great Recession of 2007–2009, when the stock market went down over 50 percent? That was your money. If you had $1 million in the market in 2007, you may have woken up one day with only $500,000 in that same account. Your financial advisor may have been saying one of two things:

1. "You're fine. Just take out your usual 4 percent and tighten your belt." Your usual $40,000 is now only $20,000. Quite the tight belt for you!

2. Or "Well, let's recalculate. Your usual 4 percent was $40,000. Now you need to withdraw 8 percent for that dollar amount. Go ahead!"

That's guesswork. You're going to run out of money.

However, if you have an annuity—specifically, a fixed indexed annuity (FIA)—in which you put a portion of your retirement funds, this is the start of a retirement income plan. Here is what a hypothetical example might look like. For this example, we'll assume a nest egg of $1,500,000, with $1,000,000 going into a Fixed Index Annuity.

- There are some annuity products that offer a bonus. If we assume a 10 percent bonus, you would get $100,000 added to your $1,000,000. Some annuity contracts may have a bonus feature that provides you with some additional retirement money.

- If the market declines (historically the market goes up and down over time), you don't lose anything— not a nickel of the original money you put in.

- The calculations for lifetime income are complicated, but for simplicity's sake, let's say your payout rate is 5 percent a year from that annuity in the form of monthly mailbox paychecks. You'll get $55,000 per year, which equates to a monthly payment of $4,583—guaranteed.

- If you die the next day after the market dives 50 percent, with all your money invested in the stock market, your million dollars is suddenly $500,000. In such cases, your spouse or heirs will get whatever is left—in this case, $500,000. Something to note in this case is that taxes may be treated differently for spousal beneficiaries than for other beneficiaries, depending on what the beneficiary chooses to do with these funds.

- When you pass away holding an FIA with a value of $1,100,000, if we assume that no withdrawals have been made, the next day, the spouse or your heir gets $1,100,000. Keep in mind that the bonus is usually subject to a vesting schedule. For example, if the owner passes away in the first

ten years, there may be a reduction in the bonus
amount paid as a death benefit.

Annuities have been around for over two centuries.
When the "new and improved" fixed indexed annuities
(FIAs) came out in the mid-1990s, thanks to the insurance
industry, they paid interest rates somewhat above the standard and allowed for growth potential. And yes, the FIA
is an *insurance* product that does not participate directly in
the stock market.

However, the big deal was that the FIA offered
principal protection. You got the safety of a fixed account
that might pay as good or better interest rates than money
markets or CDs (certificate of deposits) at a bank. The FIA
also guaranteed you, even back then in the 1990s, a sum
of money for every month for the rest of your life. These
guarantees do come with some trade-offs in the form of
annuitization, which is the exchange of your contract value
for a guaranteed income stream, or an additional lifetime
income rider.

An important thing to keep in mind is that annuities
can be complex products and you want to make sure you're
working with a financial services professional who has a
deep understanding of how these products work and their
limitations.

From 401(k) to FIA

Let's say you come to us and you still have your 401(k) account. You have not rolled it over into an IRA at all yet. How do you purchase an FIA when all you now have is your lump-sum 401(k)?

We can take your 401(k) and roll it over to a traditional individual retirement account (IRA). We can also look at the potential benefits of a Roth conversion depending on your specific situation. We help you do that.

From there, we calculate with you.

- How much would the whole sum provide in an FIA mailbox paycheck? We have charts to tell us this.

- Do you need that much with your Social Security (and your pension if you have one)? Maybe. Maybe not.

- We do the math and work backward into an annuity amount that fills your income needs.

- We can then roll that lump-sum amount into an annuity.

- The rest stays in that IRA or Roth investment account.

Once you tell the insurance company, "Start sending me my monthly check," that monthly amount comes to you like clockwork—for the rest of your life.

What happens if you don't use up the whole annuity value when you pass away? It's not like Social Security or a pension, which are just gone when you pass away. Depending on the annuitization option you chose, or the income rider on your policy, your beneficiaries will receive the death benefit from the contract. It's not a stock market investment but an insurance contract.

If your fixed indexed annuity uses the S&P 500 as its index. What happens if the S&P 500 goes down overall in any year? It's not a loss for the client's FIA because the FIA is not a stock. It's an insurance contract. You don't suffer the loss. You do, however, get to participate in the gains. Depending on the contract, there may be some limitations on how much of those gains you get to participate in–called a participation rate. They may also have a cap on the gains per contract year. These are important details that we always review with our clients prior to them purchasing the annuity.

A fixed indexed annuity is an insurance contract that:

- Protects your principal and can guarantee an income stream;
- Allows you to receive a mailbox paycheck in the same monthly amount for life; and
- Has the opportunity to grow with the market index it's tracking (up to the cap).

You are in the fixed option, and no matter how far down the stock market goes, your monthly mailbox paycheck is the same—no decrease. When the market goes up, your principal (not your monthly amount, but the total in the policy) may increase too (depending on how your annuity contract is structured).

The FIA offers the safety of the bank with an insurance contract that allows you to participate in market returns, up to a cap. Something to note is that FIAs don't participate directly in the stock market but instead are credited based on the performance of the chosen market index.

These products are designed specifically to create a stream of income for retirement.

Yesterday, we talked again with a seventy-four-year-old retired client who still had his money in his 401(k). He had done his TEP—his will, trust, and powers of attorney—several weeks earlier. He'd been unhappy about his 401(k) and was ready to talk about it. He'd had high fees, and he'd made no money. No gains. In fact, he'd lost money. He brought all his financial account statements to us to review so that we could understand his situation and his goals. We talked about the mailbox paycheck strategy using FIAs.

He finally said, "I'm confused. Let me understand this. Everybody I've talked to says the same thing. You're different. I've still got my 401(k), and it is a lump sum of cash, that's true. I'm telling you that I'm scared to take money out. I've lost money in the market, and I've got fees on top of losses. Now you're saying I can have a mailbox paycheck that I can never outlive just by having that fixed indexed annuity? That I can turn some of my nest egg into a thing like my Social Security? How can that be?"

We explained some more because, like many of our clients, this was a totally unknown strategy to him. We gave him the numbers. We showed him all the particulars of the FIA from A to Z. We answered more of his questions.

He agreed to roll his money out of that 401(k). We helped him with every step of doing this correctly. We sat and called the company with him. We decide how much of that nest egg to put into an annuity based on his income and spending. We got his money transferred to the insurance company he chose for his annuity.

Within a year, he'll start to get his mailbox paycheck money and receive it every month for the rest of his life. He's tickled because he's eliminated fees, he's eliminated losses, and he now has a mailbox paycheck that was calculated to cover his financial needs when lined up with his Social Security amount. He's feeling much better about his retirement income.

We talk to people who have a risk mentality and people who have a safety mentality. We explain how the FIA strategy has purpose to serve in a retirement income plan. We say, "Let's look at your money. We want to make sure this is what you need at this point in time in your life." You choose how much of your retirement savings to convert to the FIA; the rest can be in your portfolio and invested to potentially grow.

We cannot even remember sitting down with somebody who didn't do what we recommended. Typically, they say, "Nobody's ever told me this."

Your income is predictable, no exceptions. It's all guaranteed by the insurance contract.

In our opinion, nothing can guarantee a retiree the benefits of a fixed indexed annuity.

Are There Any Downsides to Annuities?

Now, we don't want to present only one side of the annuities strategy. That wouldn't help you decide. That wouldn't give you complete information.

The downside of those annuities is that you can only take out so much each year. There is a ceiling of around 10 percent. We determine how much you need to have every month to pay for things, and we choose the appropriate annuity to give it to you. Chris can also help address this with your investments, since those don't have a limit to how much you can withdraw, although you will still need to consider potential taxes on those distributions.

Another potential downside—your money will be "tied up" in that annuity and you won't be able to get it back. While it's true, you are limited in the amount you can take without penalty, your money is coming back to you, so to speak, every month for life in a guaranteed amount.

People fear market risk. That is not an issue here. Your annuity will not "take a dive" when the stock market does. No bear market can cause your annuity to go down. You are not in the market; this is an insurance contract. Your million dollars is intact, and your mailbox paycheck never misses a month.

A third downside is that you are not earning as much as you could by staying fully in the stock market. This is true sometimes. Because of the caps and participation rates that are built into annuity contracts, there may be some years that you don't get credited the full growth of the market index. This is a trade-off for offering you the downside protection that you get from an FIA.

As you can see, there's no such thing as a perfect product. These serve an important role in a retirement income plan and they allow you to be able to get that mailbox paycheck for the rest of their life.

Since Bostian Retirement Planning and Wealth Management has been doing this work for fifty years, we now have clients whose adult children have created mailbox paychecks for themselves, and even whose grandkids are in (or preparing for) retirement. Our client relationships often span multiple generations.

We have a lady who has been a client since before her husband passed. She was always tight as the dickens. She wouldn't spend a quarter if she could spend a penny, then she would decide to hang on to the penny. She got a death claim paid out to her about eight years ago at her husband's death. She's only in her mid-sixties now, with a $2 million nest egg. When we met her, she was focused mainly on leaving the bulk of her money to her only son and her two grandchildren. She set it aside for them and wasn't spending what she needed to on herself (much less spending on what she wanted).

When we learned this, we looked her right in the eyes and said, "We ain't never seen a hearse with a luggage rack." That shocked her. Then it shook her. Finally, it made her laugh a little.

We also had to tell her, "Listen. You have no guarantee that you'll be alive tomorrow. But you might live another forty years! Start living your life. Your son is doing just fine with his $200,000 paycheck every year, and that great job of his. He doesn't need your money. You're stacking up a tax time bomb in your retirement accounts. You should start spending your money. He wants you to get out there and live a little, you know! Wouldn't you rather enjoy your children and grandchildren now while you're healthy and strong? You've got $2 million. Spend some of it on adventures with those grandkids. Take a trip with them. Go down to Florida to Disney with them. Go play tourist across the south with them. Take them all to the Big Apple. Do some winter sports with your family somewhere."

She finally understood. She started doing that. This grandmother picked up on the term "experiential gifts." Her little experiential trips became the source of much excitement for her grandchildren ("Granny's taking us to Disney!" "Granny's taking us skiing!").

A fixed indexed annuity has a purpose in a retirement income plan that addresses a need for a steady income stream during the distribution phase of your financial life. The FIA answers the question, "How much can I spend every month the rest of my life and never run out of income?"

It was welcome news for us planners and our clients when insurance companies got together to create a product called a fixed indexed annuity. We believe the fixed indexed annuity has become one of the most important retirement instruments that we have today.

Our Difference

Here's our difference. We believe that "telling is selling." We don't just sell you a product. We are your educators in the retirement income planning space. We are educators in the annuity space. We have to be. That is because we find most clients don't understand annuities in general. Putting any of your money into an FIA is your decision. We educate, sit back, and let you decide whether it's a solution for you.

We let clients know how much difference there is between what the banks told them, what the brokers have told them, and what other insurance agents have told them. As we keep repeating, we explain strategies—including our mailbox paycheck strategy—until our clients understand. Then, from knowledge, they can decide what's best for them.

Our goal is that you have a better retirement and have a plan for your money during that time of your life. Our clients have told us that, when you have a well-thought-out retirement income plan, you can SWAN (sleep well at night). When you sleep well, you can enjoy life.

When the day starts and when the day ends, we are retirement planning specialists. We are making a major difference in the retirement lives of thousands of clients—forever. That's largely due to our retirement income planning approach and making sure you have your mailbox paycheck.

So don't resist. Don't protest. Don't throw this book overboard into the lake. In retirement, I believe, the most peace of mind you'll have regarding your money is knowing that you have a mailbox paycheck for life—made up of your Social Security and your fixed indexed annuity.

CHAPTER 13

THE IMPORTANCE OF YOUR SOCIAL SECURITY

Since we've touched on Social Security, let us say a few words about this vital benefit. In our experience, there's a lot to Social Security that people have never heard about or understood—even beyond thinking of it as your mailbox paycheck.

You might have never known it was an annuity until you read our book, and yet it is a government-backed income stream for American retirees. Whether you have already started your Social Security benefit or not, read this chapter to learn even more about this piece of your retirement wealth planning.

Collecting Social Security

Deciding when to collect Social Security benefits during retirement depends on various factors, including your individual circumstances and financial needs. It's very personal. What worked for your parents, friends, or neighbors may not work best for you. If you have not yet started to receive your benefit, consult us. We'll walk you through the rules, look at your situation, and answer your questions.

Social Security has been with us long enough that we don't worry about it during our working years. But we've seen it: At that magical age of sixty, people start asking questions about it.

Here are the ones we find ourselves answering most often:

- At what age can I start receiving Social Security retirement benefits?

- What is my full retirement age?

- Should I start my Social Security at sixty-two, full retirement age (sixty-six or sixty-seven), or wait until seventy?

- How is my Social Security benefit amount calculated?

- Is there a way to know how much my future benefits will be to help me decide when to take them?

- Taxes! Am I allowed to work along with collecting Social Security?

- How do spousal benefits work?

- Will Social Security benefits be taxed?

Get the answers to those questions *before* deciding to start collecting your Social Security benefit. We always say this because you only get one chance to decide when to start. Almost all the answers to the above questions are personal to you and your situation.

Here are some answers that apply to everyone.

Full Retirement Age

Your full retirement age (FRA) is a Social Security benchmark. It is the age at which you're entitled to receive 100 percent of your Social Security benefit amount. It depends on your birth year, but FRA is either sixty-six or sixty-seven years of age, according to current rules.

Early Retirement

You can choose to start receiving Social Security benefits as early as age sixty-two. However, if you decide to collect early, your monthly benefit will be permanently reduced by a certain percentage (typically reduced by up to 30 percent of your FRA).

Delayed Retirement

If you delay claiming Social Security benefits beyond your FRA to age seventy, this can result in a significant increase in your monthly payments.

When to Claim

All this said, we cannot tell you in this book what age is best for you to start collecting your benefits.

We have had married couples as clients who have both elected their Social Security at sixty-two. We have also had married couples who both elected their Social Security at their FRA of sixty-six or sixty-seven.

These solutions are not wrong. But these couples probably did not maximize their Social Security benefits by doing so.

If you are married, consider this strategy, which almost none of our clients ever thought of:

- One of you should take your benefits at the latest age (age seventy) to receive the highest monthly benefit amount. If one of you works that long, you are the one who should do this.

- The other spouse can start benefits at the FRA or at sixty-two.

Why do this? Upon the death of the first spouse, Social Security looks at both benefits. It expires the lower one, leaving the surviving spouse with the higher benefit. This is true whether that higher benefit was the survivor's amount or not. This strategy provides the best spousal support.

There are two other considerations about when you claim your benefits.

Your Health

You don't know what health conditions you may develop as you get older. But you do know what you're facing right now, as well as what financial situation you're in. If you look at your current health and finances, you may want to just enjoy retirement while you can and start your benefits at age sixty-two.

You should also consider the health of your elders before deciding. If they tended to pass away young, you may have some genetic conditions you should consider. But if everyone in your family lives into their eighties and nineties, then you may consider planning for a longer retirement—and elect to start your benefits at the latest age of seventy.

Other Earnings

One last consideration might be whether you have actually worked until age sixty-two. Maybe you got laid off in your late fifties and despaired of finding a new job at that age (or just decided it was time to retire). Something else might have come up that made you cease working. Whatever the circumstances, it might lead you to decide to take your benefits at age sixty-two, and that is just fine.

Consult Us

In the end, everyone's situation is unique, and this decision is personal. If you have plenty of other assets you can draw from and you don't need to collect your benefit, it can make more sense to delay your claim until age seventy. If you are married, there are two of you to consider.

Since you don't know how long you're going to be around, there's no right decision here. It is simply about your current situation and your own wishes.

Remember that your Social Security benefit is a nice mailbox paycheck. You do want to maximize it, but remember that it's going to be only a portion of your retirement income. That means you don't need to stress out about when to collect too much. It's just one piece of the bigger puzzle of retirement income that we need to solve together.

Talk with us. See what strategy works. Let us crunch some numbers for you.

YOUR MAILBOX PAYCHECK— LIFETIME INCOME MADE SIMPLE

When Raymond invented (or adopted, but we like to think of it as "all ours") the term *mailbox paycheck*, it described a *concept*. In retirement, people need to be able to count on a guaranteed stream of income month after month for as long as they live. That has not changed one bit in all the years we've been in business.

That is how all of our education and advice to our clients has evolved. That is where all our work with clients leads us, in fact.

Let's have a look at the new knowledge we've shared with you in this book.

TEP

We started with the end in sight. We educated you on the value of a total estate plan (TEP) and what that meant. We told you about the risks of not having a last will and testament and a living trust. We told you straight up what could happen if you became incapacitated without a power of attorney.

You finally understood that you don't need to be a billionaire to have a TEP.

The estate attorney we partner with sat down with you and looked at all your assets, whether it was cash in various types of accounts or physical possessions such as real estate, jewelry, vehicles, and so on. You discussed with the attorney, in total privacy, what your wishes were on all those issues. You put together a legally documented estate plan, which may have included a living trust, a last will and testament, a power of attorney for financial matters, and a power of attorney for medical and health care matters.

That was your legal and financial first step as a client at Bostian Retirement Planning and Wealth Management.

Your Financial Affairs

Next, we looked at how your financial affairs were organized. You brought us all your account statements. We examined how much money you had in accounts, what type of accounts, and where they were located. We looked at the debt you still have to pay off. We got clear on your expenses.

For some of those discussions, you sat with Chris because you had money in the markets and needed his securities knowledge and suggestions on how to better allocate your invested money and address risks.

Risk Education

All along the way, we taught you. We taught you about the various risks to your money. After understanding the risks to that money, you perhaps converted some or all of your tax-due retirement savings into a tax-free-growth Roth IRA. You perhaps had Chris suggest ways to reorganize your investments. You examined with him how to put some safe-money strategies in place with a portion of your retirement funds while still investing for growth in the market with part of your nest egg to address inflation risk.

We also taught you that we are an independent business. We are not part of one major financial industry corporation, which would oblige us to sell only their products.

At every meeting, we have built your retirement wealth plan, allowing you, more and more often, to SWAN—sleep well at night.

Mailbox Paycheck

The next risk to address was the running-out-of-money fear. We set up an income plan for your retirement, a big part of which is the guaranteed mailbox paycheck strategy. You can live to age 120, and your mailbox paycheck keeps coming in. The mailbox paycheck strategy is not about growth; it's about security. The money you've left in the markets will be used for potential growth.

Your Successful Retirement

We define a successful retirement as one where you sleep well at night. Hopefully, you now agree with us that you SWAN, especially because:

- You have implemented an investment strategy to reduce unnecessary risk while investing some of your nest egg to beat inflation; and

- You have a guaranteed income stream coming to you every month that is used to cover all your expenses and bills.

As we love to say, you want to sleep well at night. Reducing risk and having that mailbox paycheck are two keys to doing so.

Let us tell just one more story about clients that we hope will encourage you to consult us for your own basic retirement plan that allows you to SWAN. Keep in mind that no two situations are exactly alike and your situation and results will be different.

One couple that came to consult with us had recently retired. This couple started, as all our clients do, by creating their TEP with our strategic-partner attorneys. That happened during their first two appointments at our office. Next, as we requested, they brought in their banking and other financial statements for us. They were debt-free. This couple was unusual in that they also knew exactly how much they spent every month and had already somewhat reduced their expenses.

As the gentleman said, "We were paying for cable channels, magazines, and some online subscriptions that were no longer of interest to us. We just cut it all out. We were paying too much for our cell phones because we never had a family plan. We got one that was much cheaper!" Then his wife chimed in, "Do you know we reduced our expenses by nearly $2,800 per year?" They were both pretty proud of their money management.

Next, we needed to talk about "risks to their money" beyond everyday bills. We took them through all the types of risk we talked about in prior chapters of this book. They had a significant amount of tax-deferred account money to roll over into a Roth IRA. They wanted to pay the taxes up front to avoid the RMD tax bomb but didn't want to go crazy with a tax bill in one year, either. We crunched some numbers to see how much per year they could roll over without getting into a higher tax bracket. That amazed this couple, because as the lady admitted, "We never thought of the RMD tax bomb as a real thing. And we certainly had no idea how to crunch these numbers like you did for us!"

Chris worked with them on their risk tolerance and gently reorganized their securities investments.

Neither client had a pension. They knew their Social Security monthly income was $4,500 between the two of them. That amount didn't quite pay their bills; they needed an extra $1,200 per month to cover their expenses.

We showed them several fixed indexed annuity products that would allow them to invest $300,000, for which the provider paid them a $45,000 bonus, for a total contract value of $345,000. The contract allowed them to take 5 percent per year, which was an extra $17,000/year, or $1,437/month. It more than covered their gap in expenses and was not subject to market volatility. No ups and downs. Just ups. They chose one of those products.

It might not sound like a big deal, but to them, this meant not worrying about if or when their income stream was going to run out. In fact, they were going to get to live off the returns on their principal, so they didn't even need to draw from the principal anymore. That meant a bigger gift for their children when their time comes.

SWAN Throughout Your Retirement

To have a successful retirement means you're not worried about your money. You're not worried about the stock market. You don't even need to watch how the stock market is doing. You're not worried about an RMD tax bomb exploding in your face when you are eighty-one years old. Forget concerns about what the current inflation rate might be. Stop fretting about your surviving spouse not receiving the maximum Social Security possible when you are gone.

Stop worrying about the right people getting the right assets when you pass away.

There is no fear (as there was during your working years) of losing your job and your income with it. The income is guaranteed now. There is no fear of a lower paycheck when changing jobs, either. The amounts are guaranteed.

You can just go ahead and live your life in retirement as you always wished because you have a retirement income plan in place.

All our clients realize one astonishing fact: Their income is more secure in retirement than it was when they were working!

CONCLUSION

We hope that you have learned a lot from our book. We've really only presented, as promised, the basics. We didn't get too technical, even though we hinted here and there that there are some more advanced strategies available to anyone with a charitable heart or a commitment to only paying their fair share of taxes.

Whoever you consult, make sure they are fiduciaries. Make sure they have a holistic, comprehensive approach to planning your retirement with you. It was our intent to give you enough knowledge so that you know which questions to ask before making any decisions and can identify ways to ensure that your decisions are in your best interest.

You want to work with a professional who explains risk, someone who focuses on learning your tolerance for risk and loss. You want a professional who is independent and has access to a wide variety of products, strategies, and solutions for our vast financial market at their fingertips for you to choose from. Choose a planner who presents a range of solutions but lets you make the final decision.

Above all, work with a professional who is accessible to you year-round. You should not be interested in a one-meeting-and-done sort of relationship.

Our Mission

Our goal has always been to help our clients have a successful retirement. Of course, we set them all up with a financial strategy, but we know that money is only the foundation of the years they will now be living. We are proud to be able to help them fulfill all their goals for that time in their lives.

Raymond says, "Our education process helps people transition from not knowing where they are or even where they ought to be. We guide them so they see where they are at and show them the pathway to being successful in their retirement."

As you have read, we believe firmly that a successful retirement starts with your total estate plan (TEP). That's why it's always done during the first and second appointments we have with any new client.

We spoke about our SWAN cure and the TEP, where a better night's sleep starts for all of our clients. With their TEP in hand, they are already sleeping better—they are starting to sleep well at night when they think about the future.

There is no such thing as a risk-free retirement. There is no such thing as a risk-free life! However, we have measured your tolerance for risk and planned accordingly. If your working years were about accumulating savings, preparing to retire is about foreseeing and managing risks that can eat away at your hard-earned nest egg. In other words, after piling up those savings, the next job is to protect them. That's why we always look at risks such as inflation, market downturns, the tax bomb risk, and all the other surprising risks related to living longer than you expected. We need to look at risks with you before we can plan for the distribution (spending) part of your retirement.

As long as you are with us, and in every meeting, we educate you. We are committed educators. Along the way, we have heard some amazing goals and legacy wishes and have been with those clients long enough to see them achieved.

Our goal is to share our knowledge with each client. Each risk we have talked about in these pages hopefully gives you a good, solid understanding of that reality. From there, you read about how—with planning—we have strategies that can reduce or eliminate each of them from your retirement plan. Once you have the information you need, we always let you make all of those decisions. Our goal is that you know all of the options and you understand which options are probably best for you to reduce the risks.

And last but never least, we know this for a fact: Every American who dreams of retirement faces the same basic challenge. The challenge is how to ensure that money is never a concern in any aspect of life once the employer's paychecks stop. Once we have learned from you about your expenses and your goals that involve spending money, we plan where that money will come from. As you now understand, just withdrawing money from an account holding a lump sum is not a long-term plan!

We create your income plan around a foundation of guaranteed streams of income. This mailbox paycheck plan is absolutely crucial to a successful retirement. We spoke about fixed income annuities and other safe-money options with this in mind. We have shown you how we help you achieve peace of mind around risks of all types. As an investment advisor representative, Chris can propose ways to organize the money you keep in the markets so that some of it is working toward beating future inflation and the rest is in safe-money options.

Too many people enter retirement with the uneasy question: "Will I have a lasting income in retirement?" To our clients, we love to say, "Yes!" And then we prove it to them.

YOUR NEXT STEP FOR A SUCCESSFUL RETIREMENT

When you're ready to start planning for a better retirement, come see us. At our firm, it's not just how much we know and can help you achieve, but even more, it's how much we care. When you look at our process, that makes even more sense.

All of our meetings are complimentary. There are no fees or hourly bills for office visits. At Bostian Retirement Planning and Wealth Management, the only way we get paid is by the insurance companies for finding you products that work for your plan. And you know now that we're independent—not locked into one type or source of product—and can present many options to you. Then you decide.

At Wingler Wealth Management, Chris gets paid an ongoing advisory fee, which is a percentage of the assets you have invested.

We're a "you-first" company. Your retirement is about your enjoyment and your peace of mind. We're the professionals who are here to support you. That starts with the ability to meet you where you choose, in person, on the phone, or remotely.

When you come into our office, we start with a complimentary, no-obligation review. It's a meeting where we learn more about you so that we can go over what you already have in place. Creating a personal plan helps you protect your retirement and your estate by getting person-alized planning advice.

So you come in for a meeting to see if we can walk the walk, since we talk the talk. You let us know more about your finances and your retirement goals. We aim to get a 360-degree picture of each client. We listen and evaluate to see where we might be able to help. We investigate where you're at risk and we let you know. If you want solutions, we help with those too.

As we said back in Chapter 1, many Americans don't have a will. This is unacceptable because it means that your family is going to suffer even more when you're gone. That's where we begin our journey, to ensure that you and the people you love most are protected by a will, a trust, and powers of attorney.

A lot of people assume that they're "financially set" because they have a lot of money saved. But we'll say it again: It's not about how much you have saved in that lump sum. It's how much you're able to keep, spend, and even pass on to heirs. Chances are, you're not as "set" as you could be. If you spent forty years of your life working to save up a retirement portfolio, isn't it worth a couple more hours to sit with a professional retirement income planner who can help you protect that money?

We really appreciate you reading this book. May it allow you to SWAN—sleep well at night—because you have a well-designed retirement plan. May you experience ever more joy in life and an abundance of love in your family, with a long and healthy retirement.

If you have more questions about whether your retirement plan is all you hope for, call us. Our whole team is here, ready to answer your questions and help you plan so that you SWAN every night.

MEET YOUR BOSTIAN RETIREMENT PLANNERS

The Company

At Bostian Retirement Planning and Wealth Management, we've been in the business of helping people make better financial decisions and retire happily since 1976. We founded our business right here at home, in Salisbury, North Carolina.

We're not a franchise, and we're not owned by any other companies. This independence means we don't have investors we need to keep happy, so we can focus on doing an honest job and making your money work for you.

As the safe-money guys and retirement wealth planners, we've been featured in publications like *Kiplinger*.[12]

As finance professionals, we have taught continuing education at local community colleges, and we have held community education events throughout our county and in nearby areas.

As members of a community we love, we help volunteer and support community blood drives and food drives, and we give back to charitable organizations such as St. Jude's Children's Hospital.

Additionally, we've navigated over twenty-five years (since 1999) as an accredited member of the Better Business Bureau with zero complaints. Not one.

While not all our clients are local, many are. Our retirement strategies have been implemented by numerous retirees of many local Salisbury, North Carolina, employers, such as Aldi, Hersey Meters, Norendal, Performance Fibers, and Walmart, as well as the Carolinas Medical Center, Power Curbers, Belk, Novant, Ingersoll Rand, Food Lion,

---

12   *Kiplinger's Retirement Planning Guide* is an annual, special-edition print publication produced by Kiplinger, a personal finance media brand owned by Future Publishing. The *Guide* is distributed nationally through retail outlets, subscriptions, and digital channels, and typically includes a mix of editorial articles and paid advertising sections. Raymond Bostian and Christopher Wingler were both included in the 2022 edition of *Kiplinger's Retirement Planning Guide* on a page titled "America's Retirement Experts." This page was a paid placement/advertising feature in which participating financial professionals purchased inclusion; it was not an independent editorial ranking, review, or endorsement by Kiplinger's editorial staff. Appearance in the *Guide* does not imply that Kiplinger evaluated their services, investment performance, or client outcomes, nor does it constitute a recommendation of either advisor.

Freightliner, Coca-Cola, the Veterans Administration, Dillard's, Duke Energy, Hitachi Metals, various airlines, public school districts, and local and state governments.

In short, we've helped thousands of families throughout North Carolina get the most out of their money and enjoy their retirement even more. We believe in treating you the way that we would treat our own family members. That means we offer you retirement income planning advice and options so that you can choose what works best for you and your family. It's always about you and your retirement plan. We're the professionals who are there to guide you in finding your own best instincts.

When we say family-owned, we mean that literally. Raymond Bostian started the company, then brought on his wife, Linda, and their two daughters, Elizabeth and Stephanie, with their skills. Elizabeth and her husband, coauthor Chris, are still with the company.

Your Planners
Raymond Bostian, Founder and President

Raymond Bostian used to play softball with the Moose Lodge. At only thirteen years of age, he was awarded the Carnegie Bronze Medal of Honor[13] for risking his life to save a thirty-month-old child from being killed by a train. He went on to earn all the merit badges from the Boy Scouts

---

13   The Carnegie Medal is the highest US civilian award for heroism. "The Carnegie Medal," accessed February 12, 2026, https://www.carnegiehero.org/about/the-carnegie-medal/.

of America, along with earning the Eagle Scout rank and the God and Country Award.

After college, where he earned a degree in business and technology, he was up for a management position in the textiles technology industry, but his heart wasn't in it. His friends could see that he wanted something else. They brought him in for an interview to do what they did, which was to help people with retirement planning.

It was the perfect fit. In 1976, he and Linda started their own small retirement planning company, which was built to help their local community gain better access to retirement planning education and services. It was a huge success—and still is. Since 1999, they've been an A+ rated and accredited member of the Better Business Bureau. Raymond offers insight, commentary, and balanced information to every client who walks through the door. As the firm's vice president, Linda oversees the finances of the firm and all of the business's operational "behind-the-scenes" details. She has a passion for making sure the needs for their employees and their clients are always met. The couple's deep-down desire to do good is the type of thing that they can't (and just plain don't) teach in school.

Today, Raymond is invested in building a better community, one retirement plan at a time. He is also a nationally recognized retirement educator, seminar speaker, and national mentor to other financial service professionals and to thousands of his own successfully retired clients, now spread throughout many states. He has taught strategies in retirement and legacy planning at colleges, conference centers, and retirement workshops all across North Carolina.

He is the past president of the Salisbury Chapter of the National Association of Financial Professionals and a recipient of the prestigious National Quality Award. Raymond is licensed in Life, Health, Medicare Supplement, and Long-Term Care insurance.

For decades, Raymond has been repeatedly named to the ranks of the top retirement professionals in the world by the Million Dollar Round Table—Top of the Table (MDRT-TOT).[14] He has also been featured as one of America's retirement experts in the *Kiplinger Retirement Planning* guide.

Raymond and his wife, Linda, have four grandchildren and thoroughly enjoy spending time with them.

---

14   The Million Dollar Round Table (MDRT) was founded in 1927, and it is The Premier Association of Financial Professionals®. It is a global, independent association of the world's leading life insurance and financial services professionals from more than 80 nations and territories and nearly 700 companies. "Top of the Table" is an elite designation for financial professionals who meet a significantly higher production requirement than the standard MDRT membership. https://www.mdrt.org/. Qualifying membership in the MDRT is based on minimum commission and gross business generated within a year and is not based upon performance or returns experienced by any client or opinions of the advisor's clients or former clients. Each MDRT status designation is granted for one year only. All members must apply every year to continue their affiliation with the Million Dollar Round Table. Third-party rankings and recognitions are no guarantee of future investment success and do not ensure that a client or prospective client will experience a higher level of performance or results.

Christopher Wingler, Investment Advisor Representative

Christopher Wingler is Raymond's son-in-law, having married his younger daughter, Elizabeth. The couple met in college while Christopher was studying communications and Elizabeth was studying political science. Elizabeth is the firm's Manager of Client Care, but having filled various positions in the business over the years, she assists both clients and advisors in many capacities.

Chris initially came to work at the family business on a part-time basis, but after seeing the impact he was able to have on people's lives and the community, he stayed on full-time. He went on to earn his own certifications in retirement planning. He holds the Series 65 license, as well as Life, Health, Medicare Supplement, and Long-Term Care insurance licenses, and is a notary public for the state of North Carolina. He has also taught adult continuing education classes at local community colleges on retirement planning in our surrounding counties in North Carolina. He enjoys serving as a deacon in his local church.

Chris has been featured as one of America's retirement experts in the *Kiplinger Retirement Planning* guide. Chris has also been named to the ranks of the top retirement professionals in the world by the Million Dollar Round Table—Top of the Table (MDRT-TOT), the premier international association of financial professionals.

Chris and Elizabeth have two children, Cora and Bentley.

The Coauthors

The coauthors have earned a place in Ed Slott's Master Elite IRA Advisor Group. Ed Slott was named "The Best" source of IRA advice by *The Wall Street Journal*, and he is available to chat with anyone via Zoom to ensure that you're getting the absolute best advice possible.[15]

It's also important to note that we're not sponsored by any financial products. Anything that we recommend to people is on a case-by-case basis because you need to find what works for you and your lifestyle.

Chris is a fiduciary and an investment advisor representative who is registered with Gradient Advisors, LLC and also works with Gradient Investments, LLC, a third-party money manager that utilized Schwab as their custodian.

Gradient Advisors, LLC and Gradient Investments, are separate but affiliated companies under common ownership.

This endorsement of Gradient Investments, LLC is provided by an investment advisor who refers clients to Gradient Investments, LLC. A conflict of interest exists because this investment advisor receives a portion of the annual management fee charged by Gradient Investments, LLC, based on the assets under management of this investment advisor's clients. This endorsement could assist in the investment advisor increasing the assets placed with Gradient Investments, LLC, and therefore their compensation.

---

15   "About Ed Slott," Ed Slott and Company, LLC, October 20, 2025, https://irahelp.com/aboutEdSlott.php/.

These investment advisors are not affiliated with or supervised by Gradient Investments, LLC. The endorsing advisor is also a client of Gradient Investments, LLC.